List of tables

Acknowledgements

A great many people helped to make this evaluation possible. We would like to thank the members of the adolescent support team who bravely opened up their work to scrutiny and were unstinting in the help they gave us. We are also extremely grateful to the group manager, service managers and social workers who helped us in many ways and also found time to participate in interviews and focus groups.

We would also like to thank the Joseph Rowntree Foundation who provided the funding for this research, and the JRF Advisory Group for their helpful comments as the work progressed. Many thanks then to Susan Taylor of the Joseph Rowntree Foundation and to our external advisers, Hedy Cleaver of the University of London, Penny Dean of the Children's Society, Elaine Farmer of the University of Bristol, Sally Holtermann, Professor Leon Polnay of Nottingham University, Ruth Sinclair of the National Children's Bureau and Martin Stephenson of Include. Thanks, too, to Sara Mason, who meticulously transcribed many hours of interviews, and to our colleagues Professor Ian Sinclair, Jim Wade and Nicholas Pleace for their helpful comments on earlier drafts of this manuscript.

Above all, we are indebted to the young people and parents who agreed to participate in this study. Without their willingness to talk to us about their lives, this book could not have been written.

Nina Biehal, Social Work Research and Development Unit, University of York.
Jasmine Clayden, Social Work Research and Development Unit, University of York.
Sarah Byford, Centre for Health Economics, University of York.

March 2000

1 Introduction: The development of specialist support teams for adolescents

'The support worker was very positive really . . . You know, if there was a problem it could be worked at and hopefully solved.'
(Parent of Christopher, 15 years).

'They just spoke to me and got everything sorted for me . . . They just helped me with everything really and I liked that.'
(Robert, 17 years)

Teenagers represent a substantial proportion of admissions to local authority care or accommodation. Research in the mid-1980s found that 14- to 15-year-olds were, along with children under the age of one, one of the two groups who were most vulnerable to admission to care (Bebbington and Miles, 1989; Rowe and others, 1989). Although the Children Act 1989 removed offending, truancy and moral danger as specific grounds for a care order, replacing them with 'significant harm', the proportion of teenagers among those entering public care has remained high. In 1998 half of all children starting to be looked after by local authorities were aged 10 to 17, and 14 to 16 years were the peak ages among the population of children who were being looked after (Department of Health, 1999a).

Research since the1980s has questioned the necessity of looking after so many young people. A study of young people returned 'home on trial' found that a period in care had done little to change their troubled or troublesome behaviour, and that any changes were not sustained after they had returned home. Admission to care of troublesome young people had achieved little other than exacerbating the disruption in their lives (Farmer and Parker, 1991). Yet, as another study found, preventive services were rarely offered unless families were in crisis, so that they had to plead desperation or imminent abuse in order to receive a service (Fisher and others, 1986).

Diversion of this group from the care system may be beneficial both in terms of outcomes for many young people and costs to local authorities.

Although adolescents constitute a high proportion of children in the public care system, recent studies have indicated that they often receive little attention prior to admission and have identified a need for greater attention to preventive work with teenagers (Sinclair and others, 1995; Triseliotis and others, 1995; Sinclair and others, 1997). The need for preventive work with adolescents is also demonstrated by the fact that 13 is the average age at which young people develop problematic behaviours such as running away from home, truancy, offending and alcohol abuse (Graham and Bowling, 1995). The dearth of appropriate services for this age group led the Audit Commission to argue that, as adolescents have specific needs, the outcomes of work with them are likely to be improved by specialisation (Audit Commission, 1994).

In response to these problems, adolescent support teams have developed rapidly since the early 1990s. They typically offer an intensive, short-term service which aims to prevent adolescents inappropriately entering public care. A survey of adolescent support teams around the country found that most had been introduced in tandem with a reduction in residential provision and *all* had been created in order to reduce the rate of admission to local authority accommodation. The teams usually had additional aims, such as preventing the drift into long-term care or preventing homelessness among 16- to 17-year-olds (Brown, 1998). Although the number of support teams for adolescents has grown rapidly during the last decade, little is known about their work, the outcomes they achieve or the cost of the service they provide.

2 Evaluation of the adolescent support team

The development of the team

This study evaluated the work of an adolescent support team during a one-year period. The team is located in a small unitary authority with a population of less than 200,000, which until 1996 had been part of a large county authority. Indicators of employment rates and dependence on social security benefits suggest that deprivation and need are slightly lower in the city than the national average, but there are nevertheless significant pockets of deprivation with many associated problems.

A review of children's services undertaken by the new unitary authority recommended the development of a specialist adolescent support team alongside a reduction in the number of residential beds in the authority. Decisions about the future of children's services in the authority were informed by Department of Health research reviews of services for teenagers and of child protection (DoH, 1995; DoH, 1996). The development of the team was therefore driven both by financial considerations and by professional concerns about the need to prevent the unnecessary accommodation of young people in public care due to a lack of appropriate support services. It was proposed that savings from the scaling down of residential provision would contribute to the funding of the adolescent support team.

The support team was set up in the autumn of 1997 and comprised a team manager and four other staff, most of whom had previous experience as residential workers, youth workers or family centre workers. It was hoped that this variety of experience would bring a mix of skills to the team. Its principal preventive aims were to work with young people aged 11 and over to prevent unnecessary entry to care or accommodation, to support young people's return home to their families following a period of accommodation, and to prevent placement breakdown. It was also responsible for providing support to homeless 16- and 17-year-olds and providing an aftercare service. As a specialist team, it was in a good position to develop networks with other agencies, including health and mental health, education and voluntary sector agencies for young people. It was also involved in some primary preventive activity through a number of community-based initiatives linked to schools, family centres and a supported housing project.

The early work of the team developed in the context of shifts in national policy resulting from the change of government in 1997. When the team was first set up, the national policy emphasis was on refocusing services to offer improved family support to children in need. However, only a year after the team came into existence, government attention shifted from the refocusing debate to the targets outlined in the *Quality Protects* initiative and the *National Priorities* guidance (Department of Health 1998a and 1998b). In *Quality Protects* the need for family support services is no longer highlighted as a key policy goal, although the initiative's objectives regarding referral and assessment procedures are relevant. During the period of the evaluation, therefore, shifts in national policy led to a raising of expectations for work with children looked after by local authorities and with care leavers, and a lowering of the profile of preventive work.

The evaluation

The study began six months after the team was set up. It focused on the team's preventive work with individuals, namely, its work to prevent:

- the care, accommodation or placement breakdown of young people aged 11 and over;
- homelessness among 16- and 17-year-olds.

The team's work with care leavers and its outreach initiatives were not included in the research as the focus of the study was on preventive work and, within this, on outcomes achieved in work with individuals.

The purpose of the study was to:

- identify the characteristics and circumstances of young people referred to the team;
- identify the young people's problems at the time of their referral;
- describe the nature and context of the team's interventions;
- assess the outcomes for young people subsequent to the team's intervention;
- identify the cost of the support team;
- identify the services used by young people and the total cost of these services.

The study therefore had three principal components:

1. **The monitoring of the work of the team** to provide an overview of its work. All referrals for preventive work and work with homeless 16- and 17-year-olds were monitored for a one-year period, from 1 April 1998 to 31 March 1999. Information was gathered from the support team's case files on the background of 56 young people, the reasons for referral, the work undertaken and the outcomes of the work.
2. **An intensive, qualitative study** which aimed to explore how, why and in what circumstances positive outcomes occurred. Twenty young people were interviewed for the qualitative study, together with their support team workers, field social workers (if any) and one or both parents. Interviews took place shortly after the team's first contact and again one month after case closure.
3. **A cost analysis** which was carried out alongside the intensive study and included 16 young people referred to the adolescent support team.

Focus groups were also held with the support team and the two social work teams working with over-11s in the authority. (For details of methods see Appendix 1.)

All the young people's names have been changed in this report to preserve anonymity.

3   The characteristics and family background of the young people

Two-thirds (37) of the referrals monitored during the course of a year were for preventive work and one-third (19) of the young people were referred because they were homeless or at imminent risk of homelessness.

Profile of the young people

The age range for preventive referrals was 11 to 17 years, with a mean age of 14 years, while the majority (two-thirds) of the homeless were 16 years old.

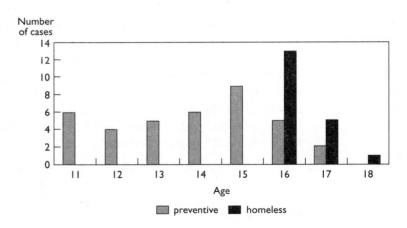

Figure 3.1 Age at referral

Females accounted for the majority of preventive referrals (56 per cent) but among the young homeless the opposite was true, with nearly two-thirds (63 per cent) of referrals involving males. Only three young black people were referred to the team, and this low number is probably due to the fact that 99 per cent of the population in this authority is white. Four of the young people were known to have learning difficulties and three suffered from chronic ill-health.

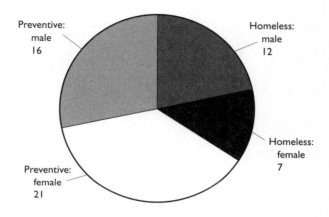

Figure 3.2 Referral type by sex

Profile of the families

Many parents had serious health, mental health or emotional problems

In half of the referrals to the team, parents were known to have serious problems of their own, which undoubtedly had an impact on the young people who were referred. In nearly a quarter of all referrals, young people had witnessed domestic violence and some parents were known to suffer from mental health problems, chronic ill-health or disability, or were known to be substance abusers. Many of the parents had multiple problems. Studies of looked-after children and of child abuse have pointed to the link between parental mental illness, domestic violence and drug and alcohol misuse and the parents' capacity to respond to the needs of their children (Cleaver and others, 1999; Packman and Hall, 1998; Wade and Biehal, 1998). Research has shown an association between parental depression and emotional problems, behaviour problems and school-related difficulties in adolescents. In particular, children whose mothers suffer from depression may show more behaviour problems than those whose mothers do not. Children who have witnessed domestic violence have also been found to be far more likely to develop behaviour problems (Cleaver and others, 1999).

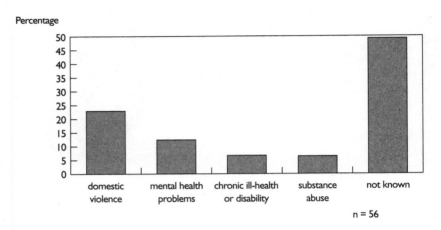

Figure 3.3 **Parental problems at referral**

Most came from lone-parent or reconstituted families

It is likely that the breakdown and reforming of parental relationships contributed to family stress for these young people. As studies of divorce and separation have shown, children of separated families are at increased risk of behavioural problems and are more likely to leave home at an early age (Rodgers and Pryor, 1998).

In only a quarter of the preventive referrals and none of the homelessness referrals had the young people been living with both birth parents. Just over a third of the preventive referrals were of young people from lone-parent families and a similar proportion came from reconstituted families. This is similar to the pattern of family composition for looked-after children that has been identified in a number of studies (Bebbington and Miles, 1989; Packman and Hall, 1998; Sinclair and Gibbs, 1998). Among the young homeless, nearly two-thirds (63 per cent) came from lone-parent families and 16 per cent from reconstituted families, consistent with other research on the young homeless, which has found that they are more likely to have experienced parental breakdown than other young people (Craig and others, 1996).

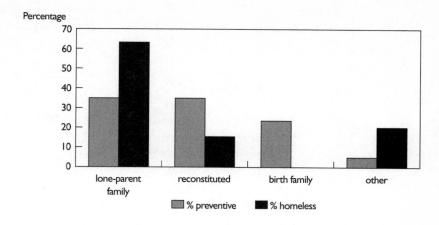

Figure 3.4 Family type

Characteristics and family background of the young people interviewed

In most respects, the pattern of personal characteristics and family composition within the sub-sample of young people interviewed was similar to the pattern for all referrals during the course of the year.

The interview sample (20)

Preventive referrals (13)

Sex   Eight were male and five were female, whereas over half the monitoring sample were female.

Age   11 to 16 years, with the majority (8) aged 13 to 15 years. Overall, they were slightly younger than the monitoring sample, with a mean age that was six months lower (13.5 years).

Family background   Similar to all referrals during the year, most lived either in lone-parent (6) or reconstituted families (5).

Minority ethnic origin   The sample included one young person of African-Caribbean origin and one of Asian origin.

Homelessness referrals (7)

Sex   As with the monitoring sample, this group was predominantly male (5).

Age   The majority (4) were 16 years old, similar to the pattern for all homeless referrals.

Family background   Similar to the monitoring sample, most came from lone-parent families (5), with the remainder from reconstituted families (2).

Minority ethnic origin   All were white.

4   The young people's problems

Reasons for referral

In a quarter of all referrals parents were threatening to throw young people out of the home so that, depending on their age, these young people appeared to be either on the brink of having to be looked after by the local authority or of homelessness. Children who are looked after by local authorities may either be accommodated or placed in care. Young people in public care may therefore be:

- accommodated by the local authority under a voluntary agreement (Children Act 1989, Section 20), often at the request of a parent; or
- placed in the care of a local authority by a court, by means of a care order (Children Act 1989, Section 31).

Preventive referrals

Although the principal preventive aim of the team was the prevention of accommodation, requests for accommodation featured in only 41 per cent of the referrals for preventive work. Such requests were made by either parents or young people – in most cases by parents. The most common reasons for referral related to problems with young people's behaviour and with difficulties in young people's relationships with their parents which, perhaps not surprisingly, tended to go hand in hand. Over two-thirds of the preventive referrals featured complaints about young people's behaviour at home and over two-thirds raised concerns about problems in parent–child relationships, but in many cases these concerns overlapped. Parenting problems were also mentioned in many of the preventive referrals and again, in many cases, these overlapped with concerns about the young people's behaviour and difficulties in family relationships. Just under a fifth of the referrals also mentioned concern about young people putting themselves at risk by running away or staying out overnight. Substance abuse by young people was also known to be an issue in over a quarter of preventive referrals.

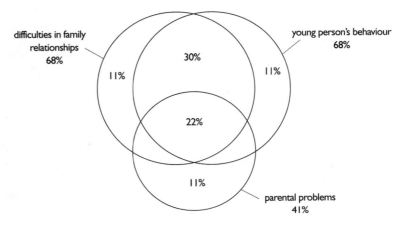

Figure 4.1 Reason for referral – preventive work

The interviews held with 13 young people referred for preventive work and their parents shed more light on the way in which reasons for referral were interwoven.

Reasons for referral: interview sample (preventive)

All but one of these 13 requests for a preventive service featured complaints or concerns about the young people's argumentative, antisocial or risky behaviour. Indeed, difficult behaviour was the principal issue which triggered referral to the support team in almost every case. Parents' concerns about difficult behaviour in the home were usually closely linked to concerns about behaviour outside, at school or on the streets. A number of parents felt their children had got beyond their control and nearly half were concerned about them putting themselves at risk because they were staying out overnight or running away.

Two referrals, triggered by concern about extremely aggressive or risky behaviour by young people who were on the Child Protection Register, were made by social workers coordinating long-term family support. A wide range of professionals, including family centre staff, family aides, community psychiatric nurses and education social workers, was already supporting these families. It was hoped that the support team could work with the young people on their behaviour and give them an independent person to talk to about family problems.

In only five of these preventive referrals was there any concern that the young person was on the brink of having to be looked after. In the above two cases, referral to the support team was one element of a last-ditch attempt to avoid care proceedings. In two other cases, parents felt that they could no longer cope with their child's behaviour and were vehemently requesting accommodation, while in another, a 16-year-old had walked out of home and was refusing to return. The team was offering an early preventive service to the remaining eight families, where there was no immediate concern about accommodation, although in two of these cases parents had requested this in the past.

Homelessness referrals

Among the 19 young people referred to the team during the year due to homelessness, 14 were homeless at referral, four were threatened with imminent homelessness and one needed support because he had recently been discharged from a young offenders' institution. Difficulties in relationships with parents were the underlying cause of homelessness for all of these 16- and 17-year-olds.

Reasons for referral: interview sample (homeless)

For all seven of the homeless young people interviewed, a breakdown in relationships with their parents was the cause of homelessness. In two cases, this had just occurred, while in two others, young people had been homeless for some time due to estrangement from their parents and were sleeping rough or in bed and breakfast accommodation. In the other three cases, the young people were at imminent risk of homelessness. In all three, there were long-standing family problems and there had been many years of social services' intervention. Two of these were care leavers who had returned home after leaving care but, as so often happens in these circumstances, the situation had broken down.

Complexity of young people's problems

Preventive referrals

Many of the young people had long-standing problems

The welfare histories of these young people indicate that many had been experiencing problems for some time, as 58 per cent were known to have a history of abuse, neglect, placement in care and/or social services involvement. Among the young people referred for preventive work, over one-tenth had been looked after in the past. Many were known to have experienced abuse or neglect and two young people were thought to be currently at risk of abuse. In over 40 per cent of preventive referrals, families had had past involvement with social services and, for some, this contact was ongoing at the point of referral to the support team.

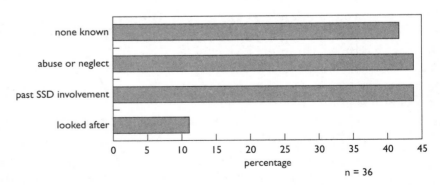

Figure 4.2 Welfare histories (preventive cases)

> ## Complexity of young people's problems: interview sample (preventive)
>
> Our interviews revealed that, among the 13 young people referred for preventive work, behaviour problems were often long-standing and were linked to emotional distress. Over half (8) of them had experienced physical or sexual abuse at some stage in their lives, or sexual abuse had been strongly suspected. Around half (7) of these young people had been displaying behaviour problems for many years which, in almost every case, had first come to their parents' attention when they were between five and eight years old, shortly after an incident of sexual abuse or parental separation.
>
> Disruptive and often aggressive behaviour at school had begun at around the same time in every case. For most of the others, problems at home and at school had emerged in early adolescence.

Many families already received services from other welfare professionals

Many of the young people referred for preventive work were already in contact with a range of other professionals at the time they were referred to the support team. In 41 per cent of the preventive referrals, a social worker was allocated to the family, although it is not known if they were working actively with the young people in question. Just under a quarter of those referred for preventive work were also in current contact with the child and adolescent psychiatry unit and just over a fifth had education social workers. Only 12 young people (32 per cent) were not in contact with any other services at referral.

Parents' emotional and health problems and young people's behaviour problems were closely interrelated

Our interviews with young people and parents referred for preventive work revealed the close association between parental problems and young people's behaviour already referred to. Most of the parents interviewed had serious problems of their own, including several with mental health problems (in most cases, depression). Some were in conflict

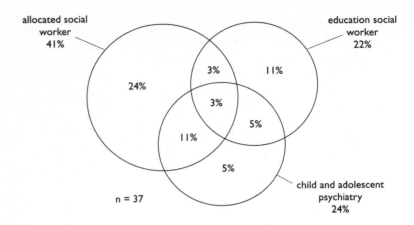

allocated social
worker
41%

education social
worker
22%

24%

3%   11%

3%

5%

11%

5%

child and adolescent
psychiatry
24%

n = 37

Figure 4.3 Contact with other services at referral (preventive cases)

with current or former partners, some had experienced
domestic violence and some were socially isolated. These
difficulties not only affected their parenting of the young
people but also made them feel overwhelmed and unable to
cope with the behaviour problems their children had
developed. As a result, six of the young people interviewed
had been thrown out by their parents at some stage and other
parents made it clear that they wanted their children to leave
as soon as possible. As one 14-year-old explained: 'She doesn't
want me any more.'

Their parents' problems were clearly a source of stress for
many of the young people. Nearly a third of those interviewed
had witnessed domestic violence and a few were very anxious
and protective towards their mothers, who had mental health
problems or a physical disability. For example, one mother,
who had severe problems with mental health and alcohol
abuse, felt that her 13-year-old son's risky and difficult
behaviour arose from his anxiety about her and his fears
that he would be separated from her. Social services staff
concurred with this, but also felt that the serious nature of
this mother's own problems made it difficult for her to provide
consistent parenting and adequate protection. As the social
worker explained, this mother's parenting difficulties meant
that:

. . . any adults trying to put down boundaries and sanctions and stuff he fights against, because he's not had that, really. So he's a self-parent and a self-carer, and he's got a mum with chronic problems – alcohol and mental health. He's trying to keep protecting her and he wants to stay with her. I mean, I think he's very scared about being taken into care full time.

Not surprisingly, young people were upset by their parents' difficult relationships with one another, or with new partners. There was some evidence that parents sometimes focused on young people's behaviour as the source of family problems, blaming them for conflict between adults in the family. As one mother recognised:

It all just gets on top of you and you can't cope. And you're like saying nasty things to him, like you're saying it's probably your fault that it all happened [parental conflict and mother's overdose]. And then you regret it in the end and say you didn't mean it . . . but you've already said it, haven't you.
(Mother of 14-year-old boy)

Four boys who displayed angry, often aggressive behaviour were still extremely distressed by their parents' separation which had taken place several years earlier. One boy just could not reconcile himself to his parents' divorce. He had begun soiling himself and displaying very difficult behaviour shortly after the separation occurred:

The reason my behaviour isn't very good is because of my mum and dad splitting up about four years ago . . . I mean, Mum and Dad have told me to get over it because my dad's remarried now.
(Nick, 11 years)

Where there was severe discord between their mothers and fathers, young people could be enmeshed in years of bitter conflict between estranged parents, leaving them angry, confused and displaying behavioural problems. For example, two boys whose parents had divorced many years earlier had been drawn into the conflict by their fathers, who attempted to turn them against their mothers and undermine their parenting – yet at the same time the fathers displayed implicitly rejecting behaviour towards their sons. By their mid-teens, both had become extremely angry young men, one with an alcohol problem and the other involved in crime. Research on parental separation has shown that family conflict before, during and after separation is stressful for children, who may respond by becoming anxious, aggressive or withdrawn (Rodgers and Pryor, 1998). Other, large-scale studies have also shown that inter-parental conflict is significantly associated with negative parent–child relationships and child adjustment problems (Buchanan and Ten Brinke, 1998; Rutter and Smith, 1995).

Behaviour problems in young people were linked to parenting style

Many studies have also shown that inconsistent parenting often underlies much aggressive behaviour in children (Scott, 1998). This association between parenting style and behaviour problems in young people appeared to be true in the majority of the families referred for preventive work who were interviewed for this study. In these families, inconsistent parenting took two principal forms. In some families, parenting was inconsistent because it was weak and there was a failure to set clear boundaries for behaviour. In most of these cases, mothers suffered from depression and some of them also felt overwhelmed by the effects of discord with the children's fathers.

In other families, parenting was inconsistent because young people were sometimes treated as children and sometimes as a semi-adult friend and source of emotional support. In all but one of these cases, parents had been sexually abused and/or in care when they themselves were children and therefore clearly had considerable emotional difficulties of their own. This pattern occurred in families where a lone parent had an intense relationship with either the only child or the oldest child in the family. In some families, this intense relationship oscillated between intense affection and vehement rejection on the part of the parent.

The complexity of many young people's problems when referred to the support team indicates the need for attention to other stresses in the family, perhaps from area social workers or other professionals if not from the team itself, to reinforce more direct preventive work.

Homelessness referrals

It was estimated that there were 33,000 homeless 16- to 21-year-olds in the UK in 1996 (London Research Centre, 1996). Surveys have found that young people under 25 are over-represented among single homeless people in hostels and bed and breakfast hotels. Two-fifths of homeless 16- and 17-year-olds staying in hostels or bed and breakfast accommodation have lived in children's homes at some stage in their lives, and a third have lived in foster placements, indicating that there had been problems in family relationships or in their parents' ability to care for them earlier in their lives (Pleace and Quilgars, 1999). Other research has shown that young people who leave home at an early age often do so because of family conflict, because parents are no longer prepared to let them remain, or because they have suffered abuse (Jones, 1995; Evans, 1996). In the mid-1990s, the Audit Commission found that parents were asking their troublesome children to leave home at 16 and other research has shown that some parents believe that reaching the age of 16 brings a change in their obligations to feed and house their children (Audit Commission, 1996; Smith and others, 1998).

Homelessness was associated with past family problems and abuse

The homeless 16- and 17-year-olds referred to the team during the one-year monitoring period were similar to the wider population of homeless young people, in that family relationships had broken down in every case. Many of the homeless young people had had past contact with social services, indicating that family problems were not new. One-fifth had been looked after at some time in their lives, double the proportion within the prevention group. As numerous studies have shown, a history of being looked after is associated with a higher risk of subsequent homelessness (see Biehal and Wade, 1999 for an overview of these studies). Over a quarter of the young homeless referred to the team were also known to have experienced abuse.

For example Nancy, age 17, had become homeless as a result of a combination of difficulties, most of them long-standing. She was distressed by the physical abuse she had experienced as a younger child and by her stepfather's violence towards her mother in the recent past. Her mother, now a lone parent, was struggling to bring up a large family in overcrowded accommodation. The family had had contact with social services when Nancy was younger and she had been on the Child Protection Register. Conflict with her stepfather had led Nancy to leave home, and accumulated family stress had contributed to her continuing estrangement from her mother and hence to her homelessness.

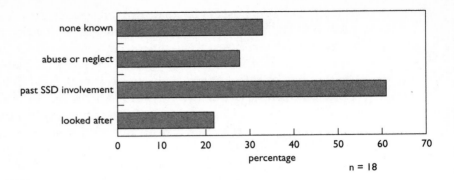

Figure 4.4 Welfare histories (homeless cases)

Some of the young homeless had mental health and other problems

One-fifth of the young homeless referred to the support team were in current or recent contact with mental health services. Other studies have shown that the young homeless are more likely to have experienced abuse or neglect than other young people and are more likely to suffer from a mental illness. Psychiatric disorders most commonly begin before the first episode of homelessness and are strongly associated with childhood adversity due to parental indifference or abuse (Craig and others, 1996). One-fifth were also known to have a history of offending.

Causes of homelessness were often long-standing

Other research has shown that the precipitating causes of homelessness are usually the culmination of a long chain of events, rather than an isolated incident (Craig and others, 1996). Consistent with this, our interviews with homeless young people revealed that problems in parent–child relationships had been long-standing, but the decision to turn young people out was often precipitated by exasperation at their behaviour, including difficult behaviour at home, offending, substance abuse and lack of motivation in finding a job. Behaviour problems had existed for many years and were usually associated with histories of neglect and rejection and a background of marital conflict. In some cases, behaviour problems had precipitated earlier admission to care. Once these young people had passed school-leaving age, it seems that their continuing behaviour problems prompted their parents' refusal to take any further responsibility for them.

Luke, for example, returned to live with his father at the age of 16, after spending several years at a residential school for children with emotional and behavioural difficulties. His parents had separated when he was very young and neither had appeared keen to care for him, at one stage putting him up for adoption. His father recalled that he began displaying behavioural problems from about the age of three, and these continued during his period at residential school. Once he returned to live full time at home, his father felt he could no longer cope with him and threw him out after a few months. As Luke's father explained: 'I learnt when he was at school to treat each incident and let go of it. But it's just been on and on since he left school ... I need a total break from it.'

For other young people, conflict with a parent and/or a parent's new partner had precipitated the breakdown in relationships between parent and child – sometimes against a background of domestic violence. Estrangement from parents left vulnerable young people isolated and without support in making the difficult transition to independent living at such an early age. As 16-year-old Ian said: 'It just feels like I ain't got no family.'

Problems were exacerbated by the lack of appropriate accommodation

Irrespective of these underlying personal and family problems, the situation was made worse by the lack of appropriate accommodation for homeless young people in this authority. Young people who become homeless often need access to emergency accommodation while problems are addressed, yet there was no emergency provision for homeless under-18s. As a result, the only alternative to sleeping rough was accommodation in bed and breakfast hotels or Nightstop, and this often involved moving around from day to day. Emergency foster carers were used extremely rarely, and not at all during the year in which this evaluation was undertaken. The only dedicated housing stock for under-18s was one small supported hostel for young people, in which vacancies were rare. Other hostels in the city offered accommodation to homeless people of all ages but this was not always appropriate for vulnerable 16- and 17-year-olds.

The local authority would only offer tenancies to under-18s if social services was prepared to act as guarantor, which seemed a little odd since social services and housing services were subsumed within a single department. Yet there were few available alternatives, since there were very few land-lords in the private sector who would accept tenants dependent on housing benefit. In particular, accommodation for young people with high support needs was not available, as the supported hostels in the authority were reluctant to accept young people who had substance abuse problems or who had been discharged from young offenders' institutions. These young people normally found themselves in a series of bed and breakfast hotels until a private sector tenancy could be found but, without ongoing support, these arrangements often broke down rapidly.

There were therefore major gaps in housing provision for young people. The authority did not have a strategy on single homelessness, which could address the problems of homeless 16- and 17-year-olds, and as a result, there was a serious shortage of appropriate accommodation for this vulnerable group.

Problems at school

Problems at home went hand in hand with problems at school, which featured in 70 per cent of the preventive referrals during the year. In nearly a quarter of preventive referrals, young people were not attending school, and five had been excluded. In total, young people were out of school due to truancy or exclusion in 38 per cent of preventive referrals. In most cases, there were complaints about disruptive behaviour at school and, in some cases, young people were being bullied. Six young people attended a pupil support unit.

Our interviews revealed the ways in which behaviour problems at home were reflected in behaviour problems at school.

Problems at school: interview sample (preventive)

For all but one of those referred for preventive work, difficulties at home were accompanied by disruptive behaviour at school. Over half (8) were temporarily excluded at the point of referral or had recently been excluded, and around half (6) were persistent non-attenders. Anxiety, distress or anger about problems at home, often accompanied by a lack of consistent parental discipline and expectations about their behaviour, made it difficult for most of these young people to settle in school and to concentrate on their work. The vulnerability of these young people also made a number of them targets of bullying, which made them even more reluctant to attend. Some repeatedly walked out of school following taunts from other children about their shabby, dishevelled appearance or about their parents' alcohol or mental health problems.

Exclusion, non-attendance and complaints about behaviour at school all increased the tension between young people and their parents. Parents were very upset and often angry about persistent truancy or misbehaviour and, particularly when young people were excluded and spent more time at home, this appeared to intensify family stress. In some cases, yet another exclusion or report of persistent non-attendance was the last straw for parents who felt they could no longer cope with their child's behaviour. Other research has shown that persistent non-attendance, or long delays in providing alternative education to children who are excluded, can reinforce other behaviour problems such as running away or offending (Wade and Biehal, 1998; Audit Commission, 1996).

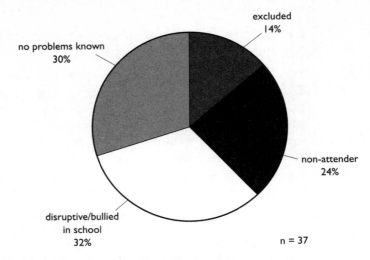

Figure 4.5 School problems (preventive cases)

5 Access to a preventive service

Managers and field social workers in the authority felt that the team's specialist role enabled it to provide a better quality preventive service than had previously been available. This was particularly the case with referrals for early preventive work, where problems appeared less serious. These families may have received just a phone call from a duty social worker in the past, whereas now they were more likely to be offered a short period of direct work. Social work staff felt that a more comprehensive preventive service could now be provided to a wider range of families at an earlier stage, and that the dedicated service for the young homeless meant that they were now far more likely to receive help from social services than in the past.

The team could also do intensive direct work that social workers did not have time for, either on cases held by duty social workers or on cases allocated to field social workers. When fieldwork services were reorganised, the calculation as to the number of social workers required took account of the direct work that the support team was expected to do, so the number of social workers was reduced. Together with the implicit drift towards a case management role for social workers in the authority and the emphasis on work on child protection and with looked-after children, this reduced the time they had available for direct work with young people. Part of this work was portioned off to the support team, so not only were young people thought more likely to gain access to preventive services once the support team was set up, but they were also more likely to receive direct work than in the past.

Referral to the support team

Our interviews indicated that although a more comprehensive preventive service was now on offer, some families still had difficulties in gaining access to support. Although the support team was willing to offer an early preventive service to families where the risk of accommodation did not appear to be imminent, it was sometimes difficult for parents to make contact with the team due to 'gatekeeping' by other staff. Around half of the parents interviewed complained that they had persistently asked social services for help with a troublesome child, but had been refused. Duty social workers had told them that they were managing well enough and that they should get back in touch if problems became worse, although these parents were clearly saying they disagreed and were at the end of their tether.

Where there were concerns about abuse, help was more readily offered. Two parents who had previously asked for help complained that it was only when they hit their child that help was finally forthcoming, while in another case help was only offered when a father said he was going to throw his child out of the family home. This is in keeping with earlier studies of the implementation of Section 17 of the Children Act 1989, which found that priority was overwhelmingly given to those at risk of abuse or neglect (Aldgate and Tunstill, 1995; Colton and others, 1995).

As the team was new, there was some misunderstanding among other staff as to the nature of its remit. Social workers' expectations of what might be appropriate work for them did not always coincide with the team's understanding of its role. The team felt that some social workers mistakenly saw them simply as assistants, or as 'family centre workers for big kids', rather than as professionals working alongside them on specific tasks, and would not accept referrals that they considered inappropriate. There was also a degree of resentment from certain field social work staff. Some social workers felt resentful at what they saw as the team's ability to choose who they would and would not work with, when they themselves had to accept any referrals for statutory work. These early problems meant that young people who might have benefited from the team's intervention were not always referred to them, or were only referred at a later stage.

Requests for accommodation

Parents had requested accommodation in 15 of the preventive referrals to the team during the year and, in three of these cases, the young people themselves were also requesting this. In two of the families interviewed, where parents had urgently requested accommodation at the point of referral, social workers had persuaded them to drop this request and they were offered support from the adolescent support team as an alternative. Duty social workers had made it clear to them that the authority was reluctant to accommodate young people in all but the most extreme circumstances. As one parent explained:

> So I just decided I'd had enough. And that's when I called the social workers in and said that it had got out of hand and I wanted him taking into care there and then ... I would have gone through with it ... but they said that they don't just take them into care any more.
>
> (*Mother of 14-year-old boy*)

Social workers felt that, in the past, the options for families might have been either accommodation or only minimal help, if any. Since the inception of the support team, they could now be offered a third alternative of community-based support, with direct work starting rapidly. Social workers explained to families that the policy was to try to keep young people within their families, wherever this was appropriate, and that the support team was part of this approach. For some families, this made a difference and the request for accommodation was dropped in favour of accepting a different kind of service, provided by the support team.

However, the reluctance to accede to requests for accommodation was not always perceived as helpful. When social workers explained their refusal to do so in terms of changes in local policy and resources, parents understandably felt that the refusal had not been based on an assessment of their needs or those of their child. Instead, parents could feel that they were simply being fobbed off:

> I says, either you take him out of here and give me a break or I'm going to end up killing him. I'm asking for the help and they don't want to know. They just do not want to know ... I'm being told, "Well, we don't just remove children." And I says ... "You're sat there coming out with all this twaddle about we don't have the space any more, there aren't as many children's homes these days

and all the rest of it." And I thought, I don't need to hear this. You
know, I didn't phone up for this.

(Mother of 15-year-old boy)

Parents were sometimes angered by social workers' use of the
concept of parental responsibility in the Children Act,
interpreting this as a reluctance to offer them help:

Well, the letter I got back from the duty social worker, it was like
a pat on the head outlining all my parental responsibilities ...
and there was no offer of support at all.

(Father of 16-year-old boy)

You just get to the end of your tether ... So I said, "I want her in
care", and they said, "You can't just do it like that, you're
responsible for her" ... I said, "I'm telling you she's not safe. So do
your job, please." And the social worker more or less said, "Well,
we can't, you know – you'll just have to plod along." ... So you're
asking for help and it's just like hitting your head against a brick
wall.

(Mother of 13-year-old girl)

Social services policy to avoid accommodation (unless appropriate) may be based on professional child care concerns as
well as on an awareness of limited resources. Yet, as we have
seen, in the pressurised world of day-to-day practice, this
policy may sometimes be translated into routinised responses
to families. In these circumstances, some social workers may
invoke the concept of parental responsibility as justification
for decisions that are informed as much by a concern to meet
agency requirements as by a full assessment of the needs of
individuals.

6 Goals of the team

The aims and objectives of the team, as outlined in its formal procedures, were:

- to help families, carers and young people who are experiencing family crisis or family breakdown to resolve the difficulties they are experiencing;
- to help young people separated from their families to return home;
- to help young people living outside their families to achieve a good quality of life.

Analysis of case records and interviews with support team staff demonstrated how these aims were translated into goals for particular interventions with individual young people. Interviews with young people, parents, and social workers also revealed the hopes and expectations of each person in relation to the support team's intervention.

Preventive goals

Goals of the support team

Improving difficulties in family relationships was the most common goal, given as the aim of the work in over two-thirds of preventive referrals during the course of the year. In just under half of the preventive referrals, improving young people's behaviour was the stated aim, but in almost all of these cases the team also aimed to address difficulties in family relationships.

The team outlined a range of goals for their preventive work on cases included in the interview sample, but the global goal of preventing accommodation was explicitly mentioned in only three cases. Since social workers only referred families to the team after they had made it clear that accommodation was not an option, avoiding this outcome became a background goal in most cases, and to achieve this end support workers were working on more specific goals. The principal goals were: improving family communication and relationships; reducing conflict; improving young people's behaviour; and improving parenting through helping parents to feel more in control.

Analysis of the interviews showed that goals were formally negotiated with young people and their parents and sometimes with social workers. In every case, attempts were made to involve young people and parents in setting goals for the intervention, although in practice a few young people claimed that they were unclear as to what the goals actually were at the end of this process. In most cases, written agreements were used to set out these goals, but the nature of these agreements varied considerably. Some included a comprehensive list of specific goals, while others simply noted how often the worker and young person would meet without specifying the purpose of these meetings. Vagueness as to the aims of the work occasionally left parents or young people puzzled as to its purpose:

> I think we both need it more spelt out, what perhaps the nature of the help to be given would entail, or perhaps whether there could be certain aims and objectives to achieve, which would actually give both Anthony and I something to work towards.
>
> *(Mother of 15-year-old boy)*

Young people's goals

For the young people, goals included 'just to get things off my mind' or 'talk about my worries', and several parents also hoped that individual help from a support worker might help their children give voice to their worries. A few young people hoped the worker would help them to get on better with a parent, and some said they hoped the intervention would help them 'to be good'. Several of the others were negative about referral to the team and said they had no hopes or expectations for the work. Some were clearly reluctant to discuss their problems:

> They say it's better to get it all off your chest, but it isn't, it's better to leave it ... it doesn't help one bit. It stirs it all up in my head again and it just feels as if it's going to explode.
>
> *(Natasha, 14 years)*

Parents' goals

Not surprisingly, many parents mentioned improvement in their child's behaviour as a key goal, often accompanied by a hope that communication between them would improve, too. Some also hoped that their relationship with their child would improve in general. These goals were sometimes remarkably similar to those of the young people, although this might have surprised their parents. For example, one 12-year-old hoped the worker would:

> Just make Mum and me be friends ... Well, I'd just like to talk to her, and if she could have a word with my mum and tell her what I've said, that might help a great deal ... that I'm sorry and that I love her.

At the same time, her mother hoped for:

> Just a bit of respect and reasonable behaviour. If she's got a problem, to discuss it, not start smashing furniture up and hitting me, or beating up her sisters ... then we can get down to the basics of trying to build up a mother-and-daughter relationship again.

Social workers' goals

Some social workers mentioned befriending the young person as a key goal for the support team's intervention and sometimes support workers from the team similarly stated that engaging the young person and building up a trusting relationship was in itself a goal, rather than an approach to achieving more specific goals. This seems rather incongruous in the light of the explicit short-term brief for the team's work, as befriending is essentially a longer-term activity. In situations where other professionals were working with the family as a whole, social workers also hoped that the team would be able to engage the young people and give them a voice, and perhaps succeed in understanding how they felt and why they behaved as they did. However, a few young people were wary of their support workers, fearing that their intervention might be a form of surveillance, because they were well aware that anything they said might be passed on to their social workers.

Goals in work with homeless young people

For all the homeless young people interviewed, the principal goal was to find them stable, secure, affordable accommodation. In some cases, an intermediate goal was the provision of emergency accommodation for those who had nowhere else to go, or ensuring that a parent threatening to throw their child out would let them stay on until an alternative could be found. Mediation with parents was occasionally mentioned with a view to this, or in order to help a young person re-establish contact with their family. In every case, these were associated goals which aimed to ensure that young people claimed benefits they were entitled to and to encourage or support them in participating in training or further education. In some cases, the broader aim of providing support was also mentioned.

Putting goals in context

The support team's effectiveness in achieving its global goals – preventing family breakdown and ensuring that homeless young people found stable accommodation – largely depended on the actions of other managers and staff in social services and housing. Any evaluation of success in preventing the accommodation of teenagers therefore has to take account of the intervention of children's services as a whole, rather than focusing solely on the work of a single team, since the actions of policy-makers and other practitioners all have an impact on the service provided. Similarly, success in providing homeless young people with secure, affordable housing was heavily influenced by the policy and resources of the local housing authority. It may therefore be more realistic to appraise the team's effectiveness in meeting its proximal goals, such as achieving improvement in young people's behaviour, in parenting and in family functioning. For the young homeless, proximal goals might include: finding them safe interim accommodation while working towards the provision of more secure housing; and providing support to increase the likelihood of success in independent living, for example, through work on helping them with income, budgeting, education and training.

7 The work of the team

Assessment and case management

Initial assessments

Initial assessments were carried out by the referring social
workers. These provided the rationale for the type of work
that the support team was requested to do and provided the
foundation for the initial agreements that the team drew up
with families. In the process of drawing up this agreement,
however, support team staff sometimes arrived at a different
assessment of the situation:

> Often what you get written on a piece of paper, that is, the initial
> referral, is quite a lot different to what you actually see ... When
> Sean [and his family] came into the room it didn't seem like the
> situation was like it had been on the initial referral ... And I
> think I was more sort of looking at what they thought the
> problems were, and asking them what the problems were, rather
> than my preconception of these other problems.
>
> *(Support team worker)*

In effect, this system meant that some families were assessed
twice within a short space of time. In some cases, the support
team's re-assessment of families as the work progressed led to
a shift from an initial focus on young people's behaviour to a
focus on parenting problems.

Assessments by duty social workers were often limited in scope

Assessments underpinning referrals by duty social workers
appeared to be somewhat limited and lacking in information
and often focused predominantly on the presenting problem at
referral, particularly in cases of homelessness. It was not clear
whether the assessment that had actually been carried out

was more comprehensive than the information communicated to the support team would suggest. In work with adolescents in crisis, an immediate response is often needed and this may to some extent account for the limited nature of these assessments. By contrast, assessments made by allocated social workers appeared to be far more comprehensive. These assessments appeared to be clearly communicated to the support team when the case was referred to them and it was obvious how the support team's intervention was intended to contribute to the overall plan for family support.

Responsibility for assessment

The question of who should carry out the assessment is problematic. If the adolescent support team were to carry out all initial assessments, they could ensure that they would receive all appropriate referrals and this would increase their ability to take on early preventive work. However, most of the team staff were not qualified social workers and could not be expected to undertake comprehensive 'child in need' assessments. On the other hand, although it might be more appropriate for social workers to carry out initial 'child in need' assessments, this may result in families being assessed twice. They may be less likely to be referred to the support team or, if referred, this may be seen as all that is needed to respond to the problem, rather than as forming possibly one element in a more comprehensive service. Also, this assessment and referral system can build in delays, whereas when teenagers are in crisis, an immediate response is often vital. A further problem is that, as a number of the young people made clear, some field social workers lack skills in engaging teenagers and can make them reluctant to accept further help.

The need for joint assessment

All of this suggests that a joint system of assessment might be helpful, involving both support team staff and field social workers, so that the team is involved from the outset. Indeed, when the team was set up, it was intended that its staff would regularly do joint assessments with social workers, but in practice this rarely happened. Where families are in crisis, the immediacy of their needs may mean that initial work is informed by only a limited assessment. In these situations, decisions need to be taken as to who will be responsible for completing the assessment, so that the work is informed by a comprehensive analysis of risk and protective factors in the family, the young person, the school and the community. Once a full assessment has been completed, the initial service offered can be reviewed and further planning may take place.

As school problems were evident in the majority of preventive cases, an education social worker should also be involved in the initial assessment. As we have seen, problems at home often contributed to problems at school, and non-attendance and exclusion could increase conflict between young people and their parents. In some authorities, education staff work directly with adolescent support teams. In Newcastle, for example, a support teacher was coopted into the adolescent support team and was effective in resolving educational problems in most cases (Brown, 1998).

The need for a comprehensive assessment

As we have seen, much of the team's work was based on a limited assessment by duty social workers, which often had a narrow focus on presenting problems. Yet, since young people's problems are so frequently multifaceted, assessments should pay attention to all aspects of their situation to ensure that a coordinated response is planned. The Department of Health's new framework for the assessment of children in need provides helpful guidance, suggesting that attention should be given to parenting capacity, the child's developmental needs and other family and environmental factors (DoH, 1999b).

In some circumstances, no one took responsibility for case management

In theory, support team intervention was supposed to take place in the context of a wider service provided by field social workers. The intention was that allocated or duty social workers would commission a piece of work from the support team, but would retain overall responsibility for the case as caseholder, taking on a case management role in ensuring that other services were provided as necessary and coordinating the work undertaken. In practice, this rarely happened. It was also intended that the support team staff might on occasions take on the role of caseholder, but in practice this, too, was unusual.

Less than half (15) of the young people referred to the team for preventive work during the course of the year and only three of the young homeless had allocated social workers. These young people only had allocated social workers if there were child protection concerns about them, if they were looked after by the local authority, if they were on a supervision order or if they were care leavers. A single duty social worker therefore had nominal responsibility for the case management of nearly forty cases referred to the support team for work on prevention or homelessness during the course of a year.

Having an allocated social worker rather than a duty social worker as caseholder had important implications for the nature of the service provided, as analysis of the interviews revealed. Among the twenty young people who were interviewed, only five had allocated social workers. There were child protection concerns about three of these young people and one was on a supervision order. In the three child protection cases, social workers worked on parenting issues with the parents as well as liaising closely with other agencies and coordinating the work of all professionals involved.

In contrast, in most cases where the caseholder was the duty social worker, the caseholding was merely nominal. Little or no work was done with the family and liaison with other agencies rarely took place. Support workers complained that they were unclear as to precisely who held responsibility for some cases and some acknowledged that in effect they had to take case responsibility, as in practice no one else was doing it. As two of the support team staff explained:

> I'm not sure whether it's been sorted out, really. If we're holding the case, then are we technically caseholders, or whether they're technically held on duty? But I'm doing the main work.

> Well, the caseholder is the duty social worker, but realistically it's me.

They were also unclear what the duty social worker's caseholder role actually was, as no work appeared to be undertaken.

Where no one took on a case management role, services were not coordinated

Where no one took on an active case management role, this led to real difficulties as no one took responsibility for coordinating the work of different professionals. In most cases, liaison simply did not take place. For example, although in almost all the preventive cases young people had serious problems at school, there was little contact with schools or education social workers. This was seen as the field social worker's role – even though the duty social worker nominally responsible was not actually doing this work. As a result, in many cases the support team did short-term focused pieces of work which addressed certain issues in isolation, for example, working on behaviour management in the home without liaison with the education service as to how they might be addressing this issue in school, or in the absence of any social worker input on parenting problems. In effect, where no social worker took an active caseholding role, the service context in which the support team was operating could sometimes undermine the work they were trying to do.

Duration and intensity of the work

Although the team normally worked from Monday to Friday, it aimed to provide a seven-day-a-week service and carried out some planned work on allocated cases at weekends. It also offered a swift response service, with a worker on call from 12 to 5 p.m. on Mondays to Fridays, which was generally used to respond to the young homeless who presented. Young homeless people in crisis, who might call in daily, would sometimes see a different worker each time they called in as their case might be jointly held by the whole team, initially at least, to ensure an immediate response was given despite competing pressures on their time. This was sometimes a successful strategy for meeting the demands of crisis work with the young homeless, but it could also make it more difficult to engage young people and ensure that they returned for further appointments.

The duration and methods of work were clearly outlined in the team's procedures. It aimed to provide time-limited support, normally for a maximum of three months, although this could be extended. In keeping with the short-term nature of the work that was envisaged, the procedures also specified that structured methods would be employed, namely task-centred and solution-focused approaches. In practice, the average duration of service was twelve weeks, and the most common lengths of service were six weeks and 16 weeks. Interventions with the young homeless tended to be slightly shorter in terms of time, but were often more intensive at the outset.

The number of contacts with young people and parents referred for preventive work ranged between one and 14, with an average of six contacts. With the young homeless, the number of contacts ranged between one and 22, with an average of seven contacts. If a case was first allocated at a time of crisis, the service could be intensive at the outset. The team sometimes saw young people several times a week, or even daily, including at weekends, until the initial crisis was resolved. The flexibility to offer an intensive service when it was needed was one of the strengths of the team. In other circumstances, it was more usual for them to arrange a series of planned weekly visits.

Engaging young people

The team's procedures specified that they would work in partnership with parents and young people and, to this end, written agreements were usually negotiated at the outset. These were followed by regular progress reviews involving the families and support team staff. This structured approach was consistent with the team's use of short-term, task-centred methods and usually worked well. However, the somewhat formal process of drawing up an agreement was sometimes difficult to implement with young people who were lacking in confidence, and it was not always easy to involve wary, uncommunicative teenagers in setting goals for the work. Despite the team's valiant efforts to involve the young people, in some instances the written agreements reflected only the parents' or the referring social worker's agenda. A further difficulty is that teenagers and their parents may have very different views of the problems that need to be addressed – indeed, this disagreement is itself part of the problem – and this is unlikely to be resolved in the process of drawing up an agreement, although highlighting these differences might form a starting point for the work.

The team adopted an informal, participative style of work appropriate to this age group. Young people were normally taken out to a café or shopping centre or for a drive, so that they could talk freely away from their families and feel more at ease with the worker. This was partly due to the lack of other appropriate informal venues in which to talk privately with young people. Staff were well aware that attempts to engage young people by sitting opposite them in interview rooms were unlikely to be successful. Unfortunately, this caused some resentment among a number of parents and siblings, who complained that, in effect, young people were being given treats for being 'bad'. Nevertheless, this informal approach was appreciated by most young people, even if they were initially distrustful. As 16-year-old Ian said: 'At first I wasn't too sure ... I thought it might cause a few problems. But once I started talking to them, it seemed fine.'

One mother, who had 'dealt with social workers all my life', remarked on how skilled the support team worker was at getting her son to talk when others had given up in the attempt: 'But he seems to push it, you know, to try and get him to talk and stuff.'

In some cases, young people would only accept the support team's intervention if it was entirely on their own terms. Luke, threatened with imminent homelessness by his father, made it clear that he only wanted help in finding accommodation and did not want the worker to raise any of the issues underlying his current difficulties: 'I told him, one word about my childhood and I'm walking out and he'll never see me again ... what's the point of getting it all brought back up again?' In order to engage Luke in resolving his immediate housing and financial problems, the support team worker proceeded as Luke wished, focusing entirely on practical issues.

Those young people who felt that the intervention had been foisted on them by a social worker or parent were usually negative towards the support worker from the outset. In these circumstances, it was not possible for the worker to engage them within the few weeks' work specified in the initial agreement. As attempts to engage these young people proved unsuccessful, these cases were usually closed within a matter of weeks. However, it can take time for some young people to trust new adults enough to talk to them. For example, one mother explained that it had taken months for her and her son to trust the support worker: 'We're not going to be so quick to put that trust in anyone else now.' The short-term nature of the work may not, therefore, be appropriate for all adolescents and patient engagement over a longer period of time might be more likely to succeed.

The team rarely suggested directly what young people should do, but encouraged them to work it out for themselves. This approach was grounded both in ideas about partnership and in a realistic appreciation that adolescents are unlikely to cooperate with any plans that are imposed on them and may simply vote with their feet. Several of the young people talked about how their support worker had helped them to consider different choices and work out their own solutions, although they had also pointed out the consequences of different choices and made suggestions as to what those solutions might be. As 14-year-old Sean said: 'He got me to work it out for myself . . . he just gave me some details of what might happen.'

In some cases, pointing out the likely consequences of their behaviour was a means of steering the young people towards a course of action the worker thought best, but this was done through listening to them, taking them seriously and presenting them with choices. This appeared to be a more productive way of ensuring that the young people gave some consideration to suggestions they might not otherwise have countenanced. For example, one young man, whose unhappiness at home had led him to take an overdose in the past, contrasted the team's approach in this respect with that of the duty social worker. The social worker had told him bluntly that his only option was to return home, whereas the support team told him that there were other options and that they were willing to support him in whatever he decided to do. Through involving the young man in decision-making in this way, the support team was able to negotiate an agreement for his return home between him and his parents, on terms he was willing to accept. The young man returned home, but felt he had had a choice and that he was in control, reassured by the knowledge that the team would monitor what happened and offer him support.

Methods used in preventive work

Our interviews showed that structured methods were used in work on many of the preventive referrals, in keeping with the short-term model of working. Solution-focused brief therapy

was used in a number of cases in an attempt to produce rapid
solutions to parent–child conflict. One support worker
explained this approach as an attempt:

> . . . not to focus on the problem with a family or individuals, but
> to focus on the solutions. So although you have to give families
> recognition that there are problems, it's about looking at the
> solutions and focusing on how things are going to work and how
> they're going to move forward, rather than getting ground down
> in the problems that have been there in the past.

In several cases, workers employed behavioural management
techniques, using written agreements to specify what would be
acceptable and what sanctions parents would use if the young
person did not comply with what had been agreed. These
involved young people and parents in agreeing on boundaries to
be set, and reinforced parental attempts to enforce these
boundaries, giving greater consistency to their responses. As
the mother of 14-year-old boy explained: 'It was my rules that I
wanted, but it was what he wrote down that made us stick to it.'

Young people were also encouraged to think about
situations in which they became angry and about triggers to
arguments, and were helped to develop strategies to avoid or
manage conflict. As 12-year-old Josie said: '. . . and she helped
me, erm . . . find out how to deal with anger. Sit there silently
and say nothing while I'm in a mood.'

Less structured approaches were also used to explore
family relationships with young people or parents or to give
them the opportunity to talk about their difficulties and think
through different approaches to solving problems. In one
case, the work progressed from work on behaviour management with a young person, to solution-focused work on
improving his relationship with his mother – working with
both of them together – and finally to work with his mother
on her own, exploring the roots of her parenting difficulties
from a psycho-dynamic perspective. However, this was
unusual, as the work more often focused on finding solutions
in the here and now or on some kind of behaviour management. In several cases an initial focus on behaviour management work with the young person shifted to a focus on
parenting skills and the worker began to work with the
parents instead.

Although in some cases the intervention included both an
exploration of relationships and the use of behaviour manage-

ment techniques, in most instances, the work had a specific and fairly narrow focus. This structured, focused work, perhaps necessary given the short-term brief of the team, gave it the flexibility to offer intensive work with families in crisis. In most cases, the focus of the work was primarily on presenting problems and did not address more complex underlying problems. However, given the complexity and long-standing nature of many of the young people's problems, it is difficult to see how lasting or significant change could be achieved by this alone, unless it was complemented by work on other issues and or by follow-up of some kind.

Work with the young homeless

Work with the young homeless was largely practical, but it also involved liaison with other agencies and some advocacy on their behalf. When young people presented to social services as homeless, a 'child in need' assessment, under Section 17 of the Children Act 1989, was usually carried out by a duty social worker. If they were genuinely estranged from their parents, young people who were homeless or at imminent risk of homelessness were normally accepted as 'children in need,' entitled to assistance under the Act. Some were dealt with by duty social workers, while others were referred on to the support team. Support workers would often work intensively to arrange emergency accommodation for young people with nowhere to go, usually in bed and breakfast hotels, and ensure that they had access to benefits. Help and encouragement were given to arrange training or further education, to find employment and to put the young people in touch with the local bond guarantee scheme. Some financial assistance was also given them to buy food or clothing.

Most of the young people very much appreciated not only the material help, but also the fact that a supportive adult was concerned about them. As 17-year-old Mark said: 'She'll stand by me ... she's a nice woman ... She's always finding stuff and helping me, you know, like places to live ... help and someone to talk to.' Claire, also 17, said: 'He's just helping me, basically. He's more like a guide, so I know what I'm doing is right.'

As these comments make clear, the support team's skills in engaging and working with such teenagers meant that they were effective in supplying both emotional support and guidance to young people trying to negotiate the sudden transition to independent living in the absence of parental assistance, and this was immensely valued. Some young people, living a chaotic existence on the margins of society, would accept only emergency assistance and would then disappear, following a week or two of intensive work. These young people sometimes resurfaced a few months later, knowing that they could approach the team at a time of crisis. One young woman, who returned to the team on a second occasion, reflected that she 'didn't bother' to make use of the support they had offered a few months earlier, but that she felt differently now she was a little older.

At times the team felt they were swamped by work with the young homeless, some of whom they felt should be taken on by housing officers or social workers. There appeared to be no clear criteria as to the circumstances in which different local authority staff should take responsibility for work with this group. Their multiple support needs and the lack of readily available emergency and follow-on accommodation for them in the authority meant that this work could be extremely time-consuming.

8   Outcomes

Outcomes of the team's work with young people and families were assessed at case closure for the monitoring sample (56 young people) and one month after case closure for the interview sample (20 young people). It should be noted that the monitoring sample included the cases in the interview sample. The study focused on outcomes for the young people rather than service-based outcomes. Changes in service patterns, for example any reduction in numbers of teenagers looked after, may be affected by a variety of factors external to the work of adolescent support teams.

Service outcomes

A comparison of service patterns between the year preceding the inception of the support team and the first year of its operation shows that there was a slight reduction in admissions to public care or accommodation, as overall admissions fell by one-sixth. The number of admissions to residential care also fell during this period, from a third to a quarter of all admissions of young people aged 11 and over. The support team may have contributed to these changes through its work with individual young people, but changes in service patterns would also have been influenced by broader changes in policy and resources.

In this authority, as we have seen, the support team was developed as one element of a new policy on avoiding accommodation in public care through the provision of improved preventive services. Like other adolescent support teams around the country, it was developed at around the same time as the number of residential beds for children in the authority was cut. The decline in the use of residential placements may therefore be as much a result of the reduction in the number of residential beds, as capacity was being reduced, as of the work of individual professionals. In keeping with these changes in policy and resources, duty social workers began to respond to requests for accommodation by explaining that they now tried to avoid taking children into care, but that a support team was available to help to keep young people within their families. In this way, the simple fact that a new specialist team was now available to undertake intensive work with young people at risk of accommodation may well have had an influence on patterns of admission. It is clear that authority-wide changes in policy, resources and practice all have an impact on the number of children looked after, so changes in service patterns such as these cannot be ascribed to the work of a single team within an authority.

In the context of an increased emphasis on preventive work, what were the circumstances in which young people were nonetheless accommodated by the local authority? During the year in which this study was undertaken, twenty-five young people aged 11 and over started to be looked after by the local authority. Four of these were briefly accommodated in crisis for only one to four nights, and four others had been remanded to care. Another two were care leavers briefly re-admitted to care when in crisis, before making a fresh attempt at independent living. In another four cases, the acute mental health problems of young people or parents precipitated admission. Only a third (8) of those who started to be looked after during the year in question had been admitted to longer-term care or accommodation as a result of abuse or an apparently irretrievable breakdown in family relationships. The support team had undertaken work with some of these young people before a decision was taken that accommodation would be in their best interests. This suggests that there were very few cases where intensive family support might possibly have been successful in preventing admission, but had failed to do so.

Evaluating outcomes for young people

The concept of prevention is grounded in the assumption that outcomes can be predicted and that interventions can alter the nature of those outcomes. Yet the numerous studies of family preservation services in the United States have found it impossible to predict accurately which of the children served might actually have been placed if they had not received a specialist preventive service, and to prove that particular interventions have produced particular outcomes. These large-scale experimental studies have had major difficulties in evaluating the outcomes achieved by specialist preventive services (Fraser and others, 1991; Pecora and others, 1995; Wells and Biegel, 1991). The contradictory evidence from these studies has shown that it is notoriously difficult to prove that changes in placement rates can be ascribed to particular interventions, so it may be more productive to focus on outcomes for individuals rather than on changes in service patterns.

However, as the studies in the US have demonstrated, it is very difficult to tease out the precise impact of any particular preventive intervention. Outcomes following an intervention may be attributable not only to the intervention itself (if at all), but to also to other developments in young people's lives. Accordingly, the ability of adolescent support teams to achieve good outcomes for young people may be influenced not only by their own interventions, but also by a number of external factors, for example:

- the nature, severity and duration of the problems of young people and their families;
- the coexistence of other problems not addressed by the intervention, such as problems at school or parental problems;
- the support available from other professionals and other agencies to young people and parents;
- the availability of local resources such as foster placements or low-cost housing for young people;
- the extent of informal support available to young people and their parents;
- the influence of peer networks on young people's behaviour;
- changes in their family or wider environment.

Where the support team works with a young person alongside a social worker working with parents, and possibly a range of other professionals, too, it is especially difficult to demonstrate the particular impact of the team on outcomes for young people. If the goal is improving family relationships, for example, then outcomes for young people are also likely to be influenced by whether – and how – other professionals work with parents and schools to reduce family stress. It may therefore be more appropriate to evaluate the outcome of the combined work of children's services, rather than the support team in isolation.

Outcomes following preventive work

In nearly three-quarters (27) of the preventive referrals monitored during the year, young people remained at home with their families and, in one case, a young man was assisted with a planned move from home. Family or placement breakdown had occurred in a quarter of all preventive referrals by the time the case was closed.

In six cases, the team was unlikely to have had any effect on outcomes as the young people and their parents repeatedly failed to keep appointments.

Overall outcomes: the interview sample

Among the interview sample, preventive work was undertaken with twelve young people. In the thirteenth case, the team was unable to carry out any work subsequent to its assessment because of the parent's refusal to see them.

- Outcomes for these young people one month after case closure appeared to be generally good in four cases, in that young people and families felt that behaviour had improved and conflict was reduced. Two of these young people, who had appeared to be at risk of accommodation in public care when referred, remained at home.
- Overall, outcomes were poor in six cases. One month after case closure, little had been resolved in terms of family relationships and family conflict. Four young people were no longer living with their families and one had spent a brief period living elsewhere.
- Outcomes were somewhat mixed in the other two cases.

Living away from home

Family breakdown occurred in a quarter of all referrals

In only two of the thirty-seven preventive referrals during the monitoring year were young people accommodated by the local authority by the time of case closure, and these appeared likely to remain looked after for the foreseeable future. Another three had been accommodated in emergencies or as respite, but returned home after only one to four nights. As accommodation had originally been requested in fifteen referrals, the team may therefore have helped to avoid it in thirteen of these cases, although other factors were also likely to have been influential, as discussed above.

However, a further five young people had left home to live with friends or relatives, although at referral there had been no requests to accommodate them in public care. In addition, two young people had moved to supported housing projects, although in one case such a move had been the goal agreed at the point of referral. Another young man, with a long history of abuse, truancy and violence, had moved to a bail hostel. In total, therefore, unintended family breakdown had occurred in a quarter (9) of all preventive referrals.

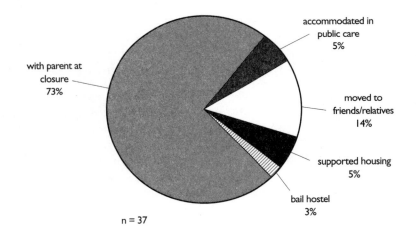

Figure 8.1 Where living at case closure (preventive cases)

Some young people felt the team had helped them to remain at home

Interviews with the young people involved in preventive referrals revealed the circumstances in which family break-down was prevented, and those in which it nevertheless occurred. In the interview sample, five of the thirteen preventive referrals were considered at risk of accommodation or care proceedings when first referred. Two mothers were requesting accommodation for their sons (Sean and Alan); one young man (Paresh) was refusing to return home to his family; and two young people in families receiving extensive family support services from social workers and other professionals were considered at risk of care proceedings on grounds of neglect (Curtis and Josie). By the time of the follow-up interviews, matters had improved for Sean and Paresh, who remained settled at home throughout the research period. Both felt that the support team was responsible for this improvement in their situation:

> Things have changed because the support team have helped me a lot ... I could tell what was going on at home and I'd have a support network with me if I wanted to leave home and they'd be there to help.
>
> *(Paresh, 17 years)*

Curtis and Josie remained at risk of care, and indeed, care proceedings had been initiated for Josie. However, in these complex cases where parents were struggling with serious mental health problems and alcohol abuse, and a number of other professionals were working closely with the family, the task of preventing young people going into care lay primarily with the professionals who were working with the parents. Although the support team's work on young people's behaviour could, if successful, contribute to the preventive effort by reducing family stress, its role was principally that of befriender and supporter of the young people.

Some avoided accommodation but moved to friends or relatives instead

None of the young people interviewed who were referred for preventive work were accommodated at follow-up, but four, including Alan, had gone to live with friends or relatives and there were no immediate plans for their return. They had either been thrown out of the house by their parents or had walked out. It appeared that, in these cases, the primary focus of social services' intervention had been on preventing the young people going into accommodation, rather than on preventing family breakdown. For example, as one worker commented regarding a boy who had been thrown out by his mother and was staying with an acquaintance: 'I think it's been an achievement for Christopher not to have to need to be accommodated.'

In the two cases where young people had moved to relatives, social workers had arranged this, yet had made no longer-term plans with the families involved. Of course, if separation is inevitable or in an individual's best interests, staying with a relative may well be preferable to a care placement. Yet it appeared that, in three cases at least, social workers were anxious to find a short-term solution to the problem of a young person who had been thrown out or who was refusing to return home. It seemed as if, once a relative had been found, the problem for social services was regarded as solved.

> It's just like they wanted her off their hands, really. That's how I felt. They were just going to put her anywhere.
> *(Mother of Natasha, 13 years)*

> I said that you can put her into a boarding school or you can put her in a kids' home, I don't care because I can't tolerate this much longer. And so they decided that they'd rather ask the family than put them into care now. Apparently, there's a load of rigmarole or something – it's not as easy as what it was.
> *(Mother of Kate, 13 years)*

In some moves to friends or relatives there was a lack of follow-up or planning

If young people leave their families in crisis to stay with friends or relatives, some follow-up work towards reconciliation, or if that failed, to plan for the child's long-term needs, might be appropriate in respect of a 'child in need'. Yet once this scenario occured, it was sometimes accepted by social workers as a *fait accompli*, which simply needed to be regularised through approving the situation as a private fostering arrangement. Perhaps, in some of these cases, it might have been more appropriate to offer support through the provision of short-term accommodation under Section 20 of the Children Act 1989, in the context of planned work towards a return home – which might involve the support team. This was precisely what one mother had requested, before a crisis led her son to walk out:

> What I had said to them was that I had wanted him put in care on the condition that this was worked at until he got back home ... I'd be there at every opportunity to work it through with him so that he could come back home and we could be a family again.
> *(Mother of Alan, 15 years)*

Instead, the situation had completely broken down and Alan had moved between various friends and acquaintances, had slept rough, and had committed a series of offences during this period. He was effectively homeless and was later anxious to return home, but his mother was no longer prepared to have him. The imperative of avoiding accommodation at all costs meant that when family breakdown occurred, young people sometimes moved out to live with friends, relatives or acquaintances in uncertain circumstances. Responsibility for this did not lie with the support team, but with the overall operation of children's services.

Some young people receiving family support were later re-referred as homeless

There was some evidence to suggest that that young people referred initially for preventive work may later be re-referred as homeless. Alan, as already described, had become homeless by the time the support team's intervention had ended, and one of the young homeless in the monitoring sample had been referred some months earlier for preventive work. The team was aware of this pattern. In one case, where a mother and daughter were locked into a cycle of conflict, the support worker predicted that problems were likely to recur but, since the girl was now 16, 'It's unlikely that she'd be accommodated now ... I think, if things deteriorated again, then what would happen is, we'd probably see her present as being a homeless person.'

Child and family functioning

Interviews with the young people and families referred for preventive work indicate how far they felt the support team's help had been effective in improving behaviour and family relationships.

Behaviour

Some of the families interviewed felt that the team's intervention had brought about improvements in the young people's behaviour. Among those interviewed, concern had been expressed about young people's behaviour in the majority of the preventive referrals. The support team was working directly with the young people on this issue in eight cases. In half of these, both parents and young people agreed that there had been some improvement in behaviour and felt that this was a direct result of the support team's involvement:

> I think [support worker] has helped us most in that it's made him listen, and whatever he's said to him – it's worked.
> *(Mother of 14-year-old-boy)*

> She's taught me how to get a bit of peace and quiet.
> *(Ricky, 13 years)*

> I'm reacting differently now ... probably because [support worker] has been talking to me.
> *(Josie, 12 years)*

> He helped me to sort out what I've been doing wrong.
> *(Nick, 11 years)*

> I think getting somebody like [support worker] to explain to Nick that I get to the point where I'm tired and I need my space ... maybe that's why it's happened, I don't know.
> *(Nick's mother)*

In all these cases, either support team workers or social workers also undertook work with parents. Other factors influenced these changes in the young people, too, as one was worried about the effects of his behaviour on his mother's health and both he and another young person had been threatened by parents that their behaviour might result in them being accommodated.

Behaviour and attendance at school had also improved for six of the young people. Three of them said that the support worker's advice and encouragement about school-related issues had been influential. Fourteen-year-old Sean explained that, because his support worker had helped his parents to establish and maintain some clear ground rules about his behaviour, 'It's just made me work better at school and everything ... cos I've thought, I can't get away with it no more.'

The support team was not solely responsible for these changes. Increased support at school and help from education social workers had also helped to improve the attendance and behaviour of these six young people.

Parenting

The support team offered help with parenting skills to four of the parents interviewed and this was appreciated by all of them. One mother of a 14-year-old boy felt that having the support team involved gave her more authority: 'Well, if it wasn't for [support worker], it wouldn't have worked. He wouldn't have done it just for me.'

Most felt that advice from the support team had helped them manage their children's behaviour better and had given them more confidence in their parenting. Particularly useful was advice about how to parent their children with greater consistency. As a mother of a 15-year-old boy said: 'I think it's just ways of reinforcing the boundaries that she's helped me with ... and strategies to lessen the tension.'

However, although they said they felt at least a little more able to cope with their children's behaviour and more in control, two of these parents had thrown their sons out of the family home by the time of the follow-up interview. They felt relieved by the reduced tension at home, but outcomes for the young people involved were less positive.

Family relationships

Some of the families interviewed felt the team had helped to reduce conflict and improve communication. Establishing clear ground rules about behaviour and supporting parents in enforcing them gave some parents greater confidence in their parenting and made them feel more in control. Among the interview sample, some families felt that this had helped to reduce tension, in the short term at least. Discussion of how best to avoid conflict through recognising the triggers which initiated it, and advice about how to manage family conflict when it did occur, was also much appreciated. In three cases, solution-focused work on improving family relationships appeared to be effective in the short term, though in at least one case, the effect rapidly dissipated and the young person was thrown out by his mother a few months later. In three cases, young people or parents felt that the intervention had helped to improve communication between them, so that they found it easier to discuss problems. Eleven-year-old Nick commented that he and his mother understood each other better now 'because [support worker] has been helping us a lot and he's made it better for us to talk to each other. So a lot of things have changed because he's talked to us about it.'

Other changes in families had an important effect on relationships between parents and their children, such as a step-parent moving out or a parent acquiring a new partner, which could have either a positive or a negative effect. However, in five families interviewed, tensions only lessened once young people had moved out to stay with friends or relatives.

Outcomes following work with the young homeless

The team appeared to be more effective in supporting homeless young people, perhaps because their goals in this work were more limited in scope than for preventive work, as they were not attempting to bring about changes in family functioning and so much of their work was practical. The team's ability to achieve these goals did, of course, depend to a large extent on the availability of appropriate accommodation in the area. Their effectiveness in supporting homeless young people was therefore moderated by the local authority's housing policy and resources for the young homeless.

The support team not only helped homeless young people to find accommodation. It also helped by providing them with support and linking them to other agencies that could help them, such as supported housing providers, education, training and medical services. Material outcomes such as the finding of accommodation are relatively easy to assess, but for homeless young people estranged from their families, the presence of a caring, supportive person who helps them to negotiate their way through crises, shows concern and gives some guidance may be a positive outcome in itself.

Accommodation

Over half were known to have accommodation following the intervention

Outcomes were known to have been positive for well over half (11) of the nineteen homeless young people referred to the support team during the year. By the time of the follow-up interviews, most were either living in supported hostels or had accommodation of their own, usually in shared houses or flats in the private sector. However, there was little stability in some young people's lives and the situation could change rapidly. Outcomes were unknown for a further five young people who had made no further contact with the team. Three young people who had received assistance were again homeless or at imminent risk of homelessness shortly after case closure.

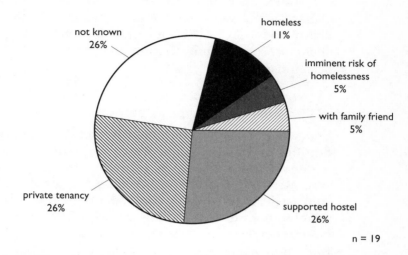

not known
26%

homeless
11%

imminent risk of
homelessness
5%

with family friend
5%

private tenancy
26%

supported hostel
26%

n = 19

Figure 8.2 Accommodation outcomes of homeless young people

Interviews with the young homeless and with support team staff revealed both the impact of the team's help and some of the difficulties of working with this group of young people.

The impact of the team

The team helped to delay eviction by parents

Where parents were threatening to throw their children out, the knowledge that the support team would help to find alternative accommodation could persuade them to delay this eviction. In one case where financial problems were an additional source of stress, the team provided food parcels to the young person to ease the economic burden on the family. As well as preventing homelessness, this approach could lead to longer-term benefits for young people, as a support worker explained with regard to one young man:

I think it gave him time to make the break away from home, but in a positive manner rather than a negative one where he was literally thrown out and told not to darken the doorstep again.

When young people were nevertheless thrown out by their parents, the support team worked intensively to ensure that they had food and shelter in emergency accommodation. Others with nowhere to go were also found emergency accommodation in bed and breakfast hotels to prevent them sleeping rough, and then helped to look for more stable accommodation.

The team provided wide-ranging support services

Some young people who were completely estranged from their families and had multiple needs were given an intensive and wide-ranging service. For example, 16-year-old Ian suffered from depression and had taken an overdose in the past, was confused about his sexual identity, had chronic health problems and was living rough. The team found him emergency bed and breakfast accommodation, helped him to find supported housing, provided him with food parcels, helped him apply for social security benefits and referred him to a specialist counsellor and a GP. As his support worker explained:

> We've taken someone who was living on the streets and found them somewhere to live, and helped them sort out the benefits and been supportive while they found other services to help them through their problems, really.

Later, settled in a supported hostel, this isolated young man felt that this help had made an enormous difference to his life: 'I didn't really have no one to turn to and then with [support worker] coming along and then getting me support here, I'm just glad I've got someone to talk to.'

Even young people with less severe problems were given assistance not just with accommodation but also with ensuring that they had an income and that they applied for, or continued with, further education or training. This practical help and guidance were very much appreciated by young people, who felt more able to cope with independent living as a result:

> He was very helpful, really nice ... It's boosted my confidence.
> *(Gemma, 17 years)*

She, like, just spoke to me and got everything sorted out for me
... If I didn't go to them or do anything I wouldn't be where I am
now, on a training course, nearly going to college ...

(Robert, 16 years)

The need for continuing support

Some young people were likely to need further help

In some instances, relationships with their parents improved
once the young people had left home. At a distance, these
relationships became less fraught and the parents began to
provide some support. A little practical and emotional support
from parents could help young people's lives to become more
stable. However, some young people's lives were so chaotic
that they were more difficult to help. Some homeless young
people moved around a lot in a short space of time, between
bed and breakfast hotels and friends, occasionally returning
to parents until thrown out again. They frequently missed
appointments, or suddenly broke off contact once their
immediate needs for shelter had been met. Some of these
young people were not yet capable of coping with independent
living, even in supported hostels. Work with them was
effective in the short term, in that homelessness was avoided,
but they were likely to require further help, perhaps on more
than one occasion, before their lives became more stable.
Although longer-term outcomes were uncertain, they knew
that they could return for more help if needed.

9 Interventions, contexts and outcomes

Despite the difficulties involved in teasing out the impact of services, analysis of the outcomes for the young people interviewed can shed some light on the question of which interventions, in which circumstances, had a positive effect on young people's lives. Although the size of our interview sample suggests the need for some caution in extrapolating from these findings, qualitative analysis of the interplay between individual histories and circumstances, particular interventions and particular contexts can nevertheless provide useful pointers to the effectiveness of different interventions.

In analysing outcomes in preventive cases, we defined positive overall outcomes for young people in terms of the key goals of the team: improvement in family relationships, improvement in young people's behaviour and the avoidance of family breakdown (where appropriate). For work with young people who were homeless, a move to stable accommodation was the key indicator of a positive outcome. Whether overall outcomes were good or poor appeared to be influenced by three interrelated factors: the nature of family problems, the nature of the intervention and the service context in which the work was undertaken.

The nature of family problems

Outcomes were positive where underlying family problems were neither long-standing nor severe. In these cases, young people and parents felt that problems had emerged or become worse during adolescence. Behaviour problems may have existed for some years before becoming more troublesome to parents as adolescence progressed, but in these cases any underlying family problems that existed did not appear to be severe.

Where underlying problems were neither entrenched nor severe, both young people and their parents were reasonably positive about the intervention of the support team. They were perhaps more motivated to accept help because they were more likely to feel that change might be possible than families who had experienced chronic difficulties. In these circumstances, the support team were successful in helping young people and parents who felt at the end of their tether to negotiate a way forward. The support team therefore had a particularly important role to play in work on early prevention, where, although families may have been in crisis and requesting accommodation at the point of referral, problems were not entrenched.

The converse was also true. Where there were chronic and severe problems such as long-term neglect, persistent and severe inter-parental conflict, poor parental mental health or parental substance abuse, the support team appeared to be less successful in bringing about positive change. In these cases, either the young people or the parents, or both, had little motivation to work with the team. Where young people were wary and distrustful, little could be achieved in the short term. These young people perhaps needed time to develop relationships with the support team, but this was not compatible with the short-term framework in which adolescent support teams operate. Equally, where parents were not motivated to consider that they, too, might need some help and refused to engage in any direct work, little could be achieved.

The nature of the intervention

Work on changing behaviour was successful in certain circumstances

The team appeared to be successful in its attempts to change day-to-day behaviours within certain families. Where both young people and parents were motivated – which was normally in families where underlying problems were not chronic and severe – some improvements in young people's behaviour were achieved through the use of behavioural programmes. Work on parenting skills and structured work on avoiding and managing conflict also helped to ease tensions. This concern with changing behaviour through the use of structured methods, focusing on surface actions and behavioural performance rather than on more fundamental

problems in family relationships, has been identified as a
trend in contemporary social work, and is not confined to the
work of adolescent support teams (Howe, 1996).

Underlying problems were rarely addressed

However, work with young people from families with chronic
and severe problems did not usually address the more
complex problems underlying their current difficulties. As
one social worker commented:

> I think they were able to engage the child, but I don't think they
> got to the point where they were focusing on any meaningful
> work because of insufficient involvement. I mean, they did a short
> piece of work and then decided they'd gone as far as they could.

Where an assessment was made that therapeutic work was
required, this was not within the team's remit. This was due
partly to the short-term brief of the team and partly to the fact
that, as is common in adolescent support teams, most of the
staff came from a background in residential or youth work, so
not all of them had training or experience in more complex
family work. When the team was set up, the intention was
that social workers would normally hold overall case
responsibility and, if work of this kind was needed,
presumably they would be expected to do it. As a result, in
most cases it was felt more appropriate to pass work of this
kind on to other professionals such as social workers or the
child and adolescent psychiatry unit. Yet, as we have seen,
where a case was nominally held by the duty social worker,
there was usually very little direct social work input, so this
work was not necessarily undertaken. We might speculate
that, in these circumstances, a focus on behaviour or day-to-
day interactions between parents and children would be
insufficient by itself, although it might constitute a valuable
part of a more broadly-based intervention which seeks to
address more fundamental needs. This may be one reason
why outcomes appeared to be less positive following work with
families where underlying problems were chronic and severe.

The short-term model was not appropriate for all families

Time-limited work has long been advocated to improve
motivation and concentration (Reid and Epstein, 1972), as

well as on grounds of cost. As we have seen, short-term interventions by the support team which focused primarily on behaviour and parenting skills were associated with positive change in some families. However, where there were chronic and severe underlying problems in families, the short-term model of intervention appeared to be less helpful. For example, in two such cases, where long-term mental health problems, substance abuse and associated parenting difficulties had led to concerns about parental neglect and young people's aggressive or risky behaviour, the support team was called in to offer independent support and work on behaviour to those concerned. These young people were displaying behaviour problems at home, rarely attended school and were beyond the control of their parents, but at the same time felt protective towards them and deeply anxious about separation.

Although a range of health, education and social work services had been mobilised to support these families in the long term, the team's input to support and befriend the young people concerned was intended to be only short-term. Yet these young people were likely to need a longer-term adult supporter, as part of the package of family support services, whose aim was to avoid care proceedings. Coordinated family support services might possibly enable these families to remain together, but were most unlikely to resolve definitively the long-term problems which underlay parenting difficulties. With their skills in working with young people, the support team might be ideally placed to gain the young people's trust and take on this longer-term role, but this would, of course, have resource implications in terms of staff time.

Time-limited interventions have been used extensively in family preservation services in North America, where intensive work is normally undertaken for 30, 60 or 90 days. Some workers there have found this approach helpful in making them focus and organise their work, whilst others have complained that, where families have multiple problems, meaningful change cannot be accomplished in such a short time period. There has also been concern that short-term models allow too little time for assessment. As a result, some North American commentators have argued that while time limits may be useful with some families, where families have deep-seated problems, they may need an infrastructure of long-term services (Schuerman and others, 1994; Besharov, 1994). British studies have also found that, where the needs

of 'multi-problem families' are long-term, short-term interventions are unlikely to be effective (Cleaver and Freeman,
1995).

Negotiation and mediation were perceived as helpful

Interviews with young people and parents revealed that
negotiation and mediation between young people and their
parents, sometimes by means of solution-focused work, were
important skills employed by the support team that families
felt had made a difference. These skills were also used to
negotiate agreement to behaviour programmes and to
encourage parents to focus on their own parenting skills as
well as their children's behaviour. When families were in
crisis, perhaps requesting accommodation or threatening to
throw a young person out of the family home, the fact that
their problems were taken seriously, and that someone
independent offered some negotiation and mediation, could
sometimes defuse a difficult situation and set the stage for
further work.

It was more difficult to engage parents in the work if their concerns about behaviour were not taken seriously

A few parents complained that their concerns about their
children's behaviour were not taken seriously either by social
workers or the support team, a phenomenon that has been
identified in earlier studies (Packman and Hall, 1998; Sinclair
and others, 1995; Triseliotis and others, 1995; Fisher and
others, 1986). Parents were resentful when social services
staff played down their anxieties about their child's behaviour
and reframed it as 'normal' adolescent behaviour. This
sometimes had the effect of making them feel undermined
and more resistant to change, so that workers found it harder
to engage parents in direct work. As a result, subsequent
attempts at negotiation met with a negative response from
parents.

Work with both young people and parents tended to be more successful than work with only one of these

Where some improvement in family relationships had
occurred, both young people and parents had been engaged

in the work. In some cases, the support team worked with both, while in others social workers worked with parents. Where work was undertaken with young people and parents at different stages, this appeared to be less successful than coordinated work undertaken with both at the same time. In these cases, there was little, if any, improvement in family relationships or in young people's behaviour.

However, where parents are not prepared to focus on their own parenting, direct work with young people may nevertheless have a protective function. It helped some young people learn how to deal with stresses both at home and at school and to consider how changes in their own behaviour might help them to reduce or manage conflict. Similarly, some parents found work on parenting helpful, even in the absence of direct work with young people, although in some cases this work undertaken solely with a parent was unable to prevent the young person later being thrown out or deciding to leave home.

Direct work was valued by both young people and parents

Direct work with young people and parents was a fundamental aspect of the remit of the team. This was valued by users of the service, who found that the presence of a supportive figure was in itself helpful. A number of young people and some parents commented on how much they valued having someone independent to talk to about family problems, who could support them in finding solutions. As one parent expressed it: 'I do feel more supported and not on my own with it.' In two cases, the regular visits of support team workers had acted as a safety valve for young people, helping them feel that they had support in coping with their problems at home and making them less likely to resort to aggressive behaviour or self-harm. As Josie, aged 12, explained: 'I can let some steam out when I go out with [support worker] ... so I can just talk about it and that ... [she's] helping me lose a bit of energy.'

The fact of social services' involvement could in itself contribute to change

Irrespective of the methods used, in a few cases people felt that the simple fact of social services' involvement had an effect in itself. As we have seen, some parents delayed their eviction of young people precisely because they knew that social services would help to find them somewhere to live. The involvement of someone seen as being in authority lent weight and credibility to young people's and parents' own concerns. One mother explained that her son was easier to deal with now: 'Just because that rule list is on the board and he's got to stick to it, because it was officially made. And because of that he knows I will stick to it and I won't break it.'

Similarly, 17-year-old Paresh felt that the fact of social services' intervention helped ensure that his parents treated him in a more reasonable manner: 'He's helped me fit back home just by being there ... the whole concept of child services intervening.'

In this respect, the fact that the team intervened at all was a catalyst for change.

Specialist skills in working with young people and the development of networks with local agencies contributed to effective working

The team's specialist remit in working with teenagers meant that they had the opportunity to develop skills in engaging adolescents. Young people commented on how they found team staff easy to talk to and clearly appreciated their informal approach. In addition, as a specialist team, they were in a good position to develop links with other relevant agencies, alongside a comprehensive knowledge of local resources for teenagers. Their knowledge of local resources and their inter-agency networking helped them to provide a more effective service to young people. This was particularly the case in work with the young homeless. In work with preventive referrals, the team's links with other agencies were not always translated into well-coordinated inter-agency work with individuals due, in part, to the problems regarding caseholding referred to earlier.

The service context

Poor outcomes occurred where support from other professionals, where needed, was not coordinated with the work of the support team

The availability of services from other professionals, such as social workers and education and health professionals, also appeared to be influential. Coordinated inter-agency work is likely to be particularly important with those families whose problems are chronic and severe. For example, in one family where there was a strong but volatile relationship between a mother and her 15-year-old son, the support worker's two brief interventions in the family achieved some short-term change. However, in the absence of any follow-up support – either by the support team or a social worker - the effects soon dissipated. Also, school attendance was a major source of conflict but, with no allocated social worker, there was no coordination between the work of social services and education. This family appeared to need a more intensive service over a longer period of time, coordinated between the support worker, social worker and the education service. Only when this particular young person eventually walked out of home was a social worker allocated.

The availability of local resources influenced outcomes

Outcomes were also influenced by the availability of local resources. The limited supply of supported hostels and supported lodgings in the authority has already been noted. Some homeless young people were simply not ready to cope with independent living without ongoing support, and as the team did not have the resources to provide continuing support to homeless young people, there was no one to guide and help them. In these circumstances, short-term solutions found by the team did not always endure.

Linking problems, interventions and contexts

Outcomes for the young people served by the support team were affected by the interrelation of all three factors outlined above: the nature of family problems; the particular interventions; and the service context. The baseline represented by the duration and severity of family problems at the point of referral is likely to mean that, although a similar *degree* of change might be achieved in very different families, the actual outcomes may vary considerably. Some young people referred to support teams will inevitably be exposed to more family risk factors than others, including the risks represented by long-term parental mental health problems and substance abuse, as well as severe inter-parental conflict, all of which can potentially have an impact on the quality of parenting and the behaviour of young people. The less positive outcomes following the support team's intervention with families where problems were both chronic and severe may have been due, in part, to the greater difficulty of the tasks.

However, the poorer outcomes which occurred in these circumstances may also be related to the model of service employed with these young people and their parents and the context within which the intervention takes place. It has been argued that any investigation of outcomes must take account of both the *mechanisms* through which a programme seeks to bring about change and the *contexts* in which the programme operates (Pawson and Tilley, 1994). Our findings suggest that the short-term, task-centred model may be more appropriate for some young people than others, namely those whose current problems are not related to chronic and severe underlying problems within their families. So the mechanisms by which adolescent support teams operate – employing short-term, task-centred models of intervention which normally focus on immediate problems – may be helpful for some families, but may be unlikely to produce significant change in others. In work with young people with less serious or less long-standing problems, the team's successes may derive from the fact that it has a clear and specific task, it has built up specific skills appropriate to that task and is able to work in partnership with both young people and parents (Frost, 1997). However, in work with young people who have more complex and long-standing problems, the tasks set for the team may be too narrowly focused, the work may take place in isolation from other professional support, if any, and it may be more difficult to engage both them and their parents in the work.

The contexts in which support teams work are also important. Changes in social services' policy and resources meant that young people in the authority were less likely to be accommodated in public care. Equally, success in work with families was mediated by the availability of local resources, such as education support services or supported housing. The availability of other formal, and perhaps informal, supports to young people and parents could also be influential. An intervention by a support worker alone is unlikely to bring about a great deal of change if other problems exist within the family which are addressed neither by the support team, nor by others, such as social workers or staff from other agencies.

For example, where problems at school and at home are mutually reinforcing, a failure by both education and social services to coordinate help to young people may set limits to the degree of change that can be achieved. Similarly, the wider context represented by local housing and employment markets will have an impact on the outcomes that can be achieved in work with the young homeless.

10 Cost analysis

Little evidence exists regarding the cost of alternative services provided within the field of social welfare and less is known about the cost-effectiveness of these interventions. Without such evidence, it is impossible to determine whether social services budgets are being distributed efficiently, that is, directed towards those services that provide the greatest benefit for the level of resources available.

Adolescents at risk of being taken into local authority care or accommodation and those who are homeless can place a substantial burden on society, often requiring the input of many service-providing sectors, including social services, education, health care, voluntary organisations and youth custody. Resources are limited and spending money on one service means denying that money to other people who may benefit from it more. All resource claims, therefore, must be justified in terms of cost-effectiveness as well as benefits to the young people involved. Economic evaluations involve the systematic identification, measurement and comparison of the costs and the outcomes of alternative interventions, providing information to enable priorities to be set and resources to be allocated efficiently between competing services (Drummond and others, 1997).

Given the lack of a control group in this study and the small sample size, a full economic evaluation was not possible. A cost analysis, however, will help to guide future evaluations and, by taking a broad perspective, enable each individual service-providing sector to assess their relative contributions to the total cost of care packages for these groups of young people.

Methods

Sixteen young people from the intensive sample were included in the cost analysis. Twelve were prevention cases and four were homelessness cases. Four of the intensive sample were unavailable at follow-up and were excluded from the cost analysis.

Information on the use of all social, education, health, youth custody and voluntary services was collected from the parents and young people at the follow-up interview, using a questionnaire designed for the purposes of the study. Information on contact with the support team was recorded on time sheets routinely completed by all members of the team which detailed the number of hours spent on allocated cases and the time spent on other activities, such as training, supervision, administration and annual leave. All resource-use data covered the period from initial contact with the support team to the date of follow-up interview.

The unit costs of services used were for the financial year 1998/99 and were derived from a number of different sources, including service providers, calculation from relevant salary scales and national publications. For more information on methods and unit costs, see Appendix 1.

Results

Resources used

The average number of support team worker hours per case was 31, although this hides a relatively large difference between the two case types. Prevention cases on average received greater input from the support team than did the homelessness cases over the period between initial contact with the support team and case closure (33 and 26 hours, respectively). However, there was greater variability in support team input for the homeless, with the total number of hours ranging from nine to 63, as compared to 21 to 57 for the prevention cases.

Other social services used included social work contact and the provision of supported accommodation. The prevention cases on average had more contact with social workers outside of the support team than the homelessness cases, although the number for both was small (three versus one contact). Supported accommodation was a service used by three out of the four homelessness cases (average 49 days) but none of the prevention cases. Foster and residential care were not used by any of the young people over the study period.

The main aims of the support team are to prevent unnecessary entry into local authority care or accommodation and to prevent homelessness. These findings on accommodation seem to suggest that the support team was successful in achieving both of these aims. Three out of the four homeless young people were placed in supported accommodation, although one was later evicted, whilst the fourth moved to a shared flat in the private sector. None of the prevention cases were accommodated, although four did leave home during the period of the trial and moved out to stay with friends or alternative family members.

School-based education services were used extensively by the prevention group, whilst training schemes and college-based services were used more by the homeless. The average age of the prevention group was 14 years, as compared to 17 years in the homelessness group, thus these findings reflect the age difference between the two groups and the likelihood of the prevention group still being at school. Six young people in the prevention group (50 per cent) were receiving either classroom support within a mainstream school or were attending special needs classes provided by a pupil support unit, often in addition to contact with education social workers or educational psychologists. In total, eight young people in the prevention group (66.7 per cent) were receiving some form of educational support at school. This finding highlights the fact that children at risk of entry into care tend to be suffering from a range of problems, outside as well as inside their family home.

National health services were used to a greater extent by the homeless than the prevention cases, suggesting a lower health-related quality of life in this group of young people. Of the major health care interventions, only the homeless required in-patient stays and out-patient appointments which were the result of one suicide attempt and one accident requiring surgery. In contrast, the prevention group made greater use of accident and emergency services with five young people attending hospital following either a fight (three young people) or an accident (two young people). Only one young person from the homelessness group required an accident and emergency attendance and this was due to an accident.

Voluntary services were not used by the homelessness group and were rarely accessed by the prevention group, with only two young people contacting an organisation that provides a youth advice and counselling service. This finding may reflect the large number of agencies already involved in providing support for these young people and their families.

One young person in the homelessness group spent time in youth custody and had contact with youth custody social workers. None of the prevention group spent time in custody during the study period.

Figures 10.1 and 10.2 detail the mean use of services by all young people in the study and by status, respectively (see Appendix 2).

Total cost of care packages

The average length of time spent in the study was just over 22 weeks for all young people (range 12 to 42 weeks). By status, the average length of time in the study was higher for homelessness cases than prevention cases (24 and 22 weeks, respectively), thus, for comparison, costs per week are reported as well as total costs of care packages over the study period as a whole.

The average cost of the support team from initial interview to case closure was found to be approximately £1,100, or £55 per week, per young person. Prevention cases were more expensive than homelessness cases, costing approximately £1,170 (or £61 per week) as compared to £930 (or £39 per week) per young person. This difference reflects the greater average number of support team worker hours devoted to prevention cases.

Social services were found to carry the greatest cost burden, contributing over 50 per cent of the total costs of caring for this group of young people, with the support team accounting for the majority of this expenditure (85 per cent overall: 96 per cent in the prevention group and 59 per cent in the homelessness group).

The education sector was responsible for a significant proportion of the total cost of the prevention group (46 per cent) but contributed little to the homelessness group (7 per cent) who were, on average, older and less likely to be in school. Costs to the National Health Service, as a proportion of total costs, were much higher in the homelessness group (18

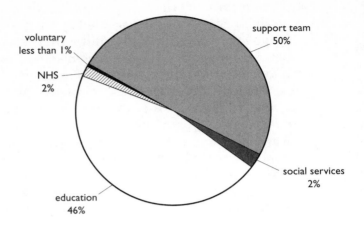

Figure 10.1 Total cost of care packages – preventive cases

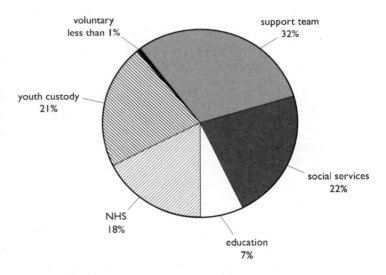

Figure 10.2 Total cost of care packages – homeless cases

per cent) than the prevention group (2 per cent), as were costs to the youth custody sector (21 per cent and 0 per cent, respectively). The voluntary sector accounted for less than 1 per cent of the total costs of care in both groups.

The total cost of care packages to all sectors during the period of contact with the support team was calculated to be approximately £2,500 per young person (or £125 per week). Despite the lower cost of the support team input, the homeless young people were found to be relatively more expensive than the prevention group over the period of the study, costing a total of £2,900 compared to £2,350. In part, this difference reflects the higher cost of supported accommodation, health services and youth custody input in this group. However, it also reflects the fact that the homelessness group spent longer in the study on average. Calculation of a cost per week removes the influence of this difference in duration and demonstrates that, on average, the cost of the two groups differed little with the homeless costing £129 per week as compared to £123 per week for the prevention group.

Tables 3 and 4 on p. 97 report the average cost of packages of care by sector from initial contact with the support team to final interview and the average cost per week, respectively.

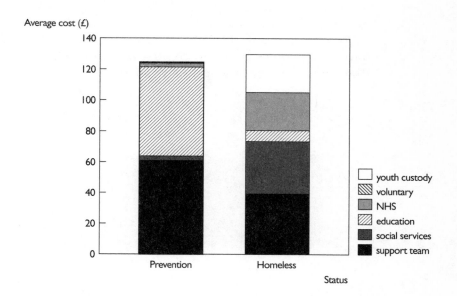

Figure 10.3 Average cost per week (preventive and homeless cases)

Discussion

Over the one-year monitoring period, the support team accepted and worked with 37 prevention referrals and 19 homelessness referrals. Extrapolating the cost data, the estimated cost of these referrals to society would be almost £150,000, of which £75,000 would be borne by social services departments. Although this may appear to be a large sum of money, the figure is meaningless without a baseline against which to make a comparison and without the inclusion of evidence of effectiveness. A full economic evaluation would provide the information necessary to determine not only how much more or less expensive support teams are in comparison to alternative support services, such as mainstream services, but also whether or not they are more cost-effective, that is generate greater benefits for the level of resources available or the same level of benefits at lower cost.

This cost analysis provides valuable budgetary information for service-providing sectors, particularly for social services departments considering the development of a similar service. In addition, it highlights the multidimensional nature of the problems facing this group of young people and thus the need for support from, and collaboration between, a number of different agencies. It does not, however, provide evidence to guide the choice between competing alternative services and therefore further research is needed.

11 Working with teenagers

Reasons for referral and service streams

Earlier studies of children who are looked after by local authorities have classified them in terms of their reasons for admission as *protected* or *disaffected* (Farmer and Parker, 1991), or as *victims*, *villains* or *volunteered* (Packman and others, 1996). In the context of the emphasis in the Children Act on preventive support and services to families with 'children in need,' these classifications might also be helpful in delineating the ways in which adolescents come to the attention of preventive services.

Those whose behaviour problems at home precipitate referral to social services, the so-called 'villains', and those for whom accommodation has been requested but not provided, the 'volunteered', may receive preventive services from an adolescent support team. For both of these groups, problems in behaviour and in family relationships are most likely to have led to their referral to social services. Those 'villains' whose offending brings them to the attention of social services may be seen by youth offending teams. Finally, the 'victims' of abuse or neglect are likely to be allocated to field social workers, although support teams may make some input on specific pieces of work.

Age is a significant factor determining the nature of the service that children and young people receive. Young people who might have been regarded as 'victims' at an earlier stage in their lives may find themselves in the service stream allotted to 'villains' or 'volunteered' once they reach adolescence and their behaviour becomes more difficult. Later still, if preventive work has perhaps kept the 'villains'/'volunteered' out of local authority accommodation, family breakdown might occur shortly after they reach school-leaving age, as we have seen.

At this point, adolescent support teams again have a role to play, this time in preventing homelessness, but they will offer a qualitatively different service to the one offered to young people referred for preventive work. If family breakdown occurs once young people have left school, they are unlikely to receive a service which addresses family-based problems and are more likely to be dealt with as a homeless person whose primary need is for housing and associated support.

For many young people, therefore, age and the immediate reason for referral determine which service stream they enter and this, in turn, determines the nature of the service they receive. For example, research in the United States on abused adolescents has shown that, while adolescents are more physically durable than younger children, they tend to display other effects of abuse, such as self-harm, depression, running away or offending (Rees and Stein, 1997). Those who internalise their distress through self-harm or depression may come to the attention of child and adolescent psychiatric services or social workers, while those who externalise it through disruptive or aggressive behaviour, running away or offending, may find themselves referred to adolescent support teams or youth offending teams. The former may receive a service which, among other things, might attempt to address underlying family problems. In contrast, those who display difficult behaviour at home may be helped by adolescent support teams who carry out short-term interventions which focus on changing observable aspects of behaviour through solution-focused or similar task-centred work.

Working with homeless 16- and 17-year-olds

Homeless young people under the age of 18 may be entitled to help under the Housing Act 1996 and under the Children Act 1989, but it is their first point of contact with local authority staff which may determine the nature of the service they subsequently receive. Despite the fact that, in the authority studied, the social services and housing services were incorporated into a single department, it remained unclear where responsibility lay for work with homeless 16- and 17-year-olds. Whether young people who were homeless, or threatened with homelessness, were accepted as 'vulnerable' and therefore 'in priority need' under Section 14 (10) of the Housing Act 1996, or as 'children in need' entitled to assistance under

Section 17 of the Children Act 1989, appeared to be a somewhat hit-and-miss affair. Homeless young people might be assessed as being 'in priority need' by housing caseworkers, or referred to social services for assessment as a 'child in need' by a duty social worker, after which they might receive help from the support team or duty social workers. Alternatively, as we found, housing officers might occasionally decide they were not entitled to help on grounds of 'vulnerability', but then fail to direct them to social services for assessment as a 'child in need'.

The work of the support team was hampered by the lack of sufficient housing provision in the city to meet the needs of homeless young people. As a result, the support team found themselves spending a lot of time looking for emergency accommodation and longer-term private sector housing for homeless young people. This time-consuming activity might properly be regarded as the work of housing officers and was no doubt duplicating the work that these officers were doing for other homeless people in the city. This work reduced the time the team had available to deploy their skills in preventive work and in providing wider support both to care leavers and the young homeless. The development of uniform assessment procedures across the authority would avoid the need for distressed young people to deal first with housing officers before being referred on for a further assessment by social services officers. Joint assessment by social services and housing staff might not only avoid wasteful duplication of effort, but would also make it easier to clarify roles and responsibilities in respect of finding accommodation and providing support.

The Children Act 1989 provided a safety net for homeless 16- and 17-year-olds in setting out the responsibilities of local authorities to meet the housing and support needs of this group. It was positive that, in this authority, homeless under-18s who were genuinely estranged from parents or at imminent risk of homelessness were normally assessed by social services as 'children in need' under Section 17 of the Children Act, giving them entitlement to a preventive service. However, it was less positive that the authority was reluctant to use its powers to provide accommodation for homeless 16- and 17-year-olds. Section 20 (3) of the Children Act states that:

> Every local authority shall provide accommodation for any child in need in their area who has reached the age of 16 and whose welfare the authority judges is likely to be seriously prejudiced if they do not provide him with accommodation.

Yet in this authority it was local policy not to look after homeless 16- and 17-year-olds by accommodating them under Section 20.

It is probable that this local authority is not alone in seeking to avoid providing accommodation for homeless 16- and 17-year-olds since, in financial terms, Section 20 of the Children Act presents a disincentive to local authorities to accommodate homeless young people. Anyone looked after beyond the age of 16 for a continuous period of twenty-four hours is subsequently entitled to the more extensive ongoing support afforded to care leavers up to the age of 21 (under Section 24 of the Act). In the authority studied, the outcome of this policy of avoiding Section 20 provision was that vulnerable young people who were homeless were placed in bed and breakfast hotels and, in most cases, had no longer-term alternative than to look for unsupported accommodation in the private sector. Bed and breakfast accommodation was paid for under Section 17, the family support provisions of the Children Act, and then reclaimed via Housing Benefit. However great their ongoing support needs, these young people were not entitled to continuing support. Policy decisions about the level of support they would receive appeared to be resource-driven rather than needs-led. It seems likely that lack of finance was a major constraint on work with the young homeless, leading to a policy driven by concerns about 'gatekeeping'.

Yet with the performance targets for work with care leavers set by the Quality Protects initiative and the proposed new duties towards care leavers in the forthcoming legislation – the Children (Leaving Care) Act expected in 2001 – there is a danger that resources will be targeted exclusively at care leavers, to the detriment of those homeless 16- and 17-year-olds who have not been looked after beyond their sixteenth birthday. As we have seen, some of the homeless young people had significant support needs. Some had suffered abuse and some had been looked after when they were younger. Some had mental health problems and others were involved in offending. Over half had had support from social services in the past, which may have prevented them being separated from their families. Despite this support, at or shortly after school-leaving age, some parents were no longer willing to let their children remain at home and/or the young people concerned were anxious to leave unhappy or abusive family situations. Paradoxically, where family support services delay family breakdown and successfully prevent the accommodation of those under the age of 16, young people may later be denied accommodation in a supported environment and ongoing support just when they need it most.

Of course, not all the young homeless would need supported accommodation and continuing support. The team felt that, although some were highly vulnerable and in need of intensive support, in overall terms the young homeless were better able to cope with living independently than many care leavers, particularly in comparison with those care leavers leaving residential placements. Some received a degree of support from parents once they had left home and some were already settled in further education or training. By extending their support under Section 20 of the Children Act 1989 to those young homeless who need it, local authorities are unlikely to be swamped by a demand for resources. Young people with fewer support needs could still be helped under Section 17 of the Children Act.

Some authorities have addressed these problems through the development of a single homelessness strategy, which pays specific attention to the needs of the young homeless, including both homeless 16- and 17-year-olds and young people leaving care. In line with current policy approaches which recommend 'joined-up solutions' in response to problems of social exclusion, agencies should work together to develop such a strategy. This process should involve social services and housing authorities, together with other relevant agencies such as housing associations, education, careers, mental health and probation services as well as voluntary sector agencies for children. Research in the field of youth homelessness suggests that any such strategy should be based on a local audit of need to determine the level of unmet need among homeless 16- and 17-year-olds in the community and assist planning. It also recommends the development of appropriate accommodation options for this group, including 'emergency access' hostels where work could be done to resolve some of the reasons for leaving home, and supported follow-on accommodation for those who need it (McCluskey, 1993; Kay, 1994). These could be provided in partnership with housing associations and other voluntary sector agencies and could be available to those homeless young people who are not yet ready to manage independent living, as well as to care leavers.

The strategy could ensure a consistent approach to assessment and could involve the development of joint assessment by housing and social services staff to ensure that responsibilities regarding the provision of accommodation and the provision of support are clarified. Within this framework, adequately resourced adolescent support teams would have an important role to play, as they have the specialist skills and experience in working with this age group as well as the knowledge of local resources necessary to provide a coherent, effective and responsive service to homeless 16- and 17-year-olds.

Models of service

The short-term, task-centred model

The support team normally employed short-term, task-centred methods and in most cases the focus of its work was on immediate problems. Analysis of outcomes for the young people interviewed for this study suggests that this approach was successful in certain circumstances, but not in others.

- Short-term, structured interventions may work well with families who are motivated to change and therefore want to make the intervention 'work'. In this study, these tended to be families without chronic and severe problems who felt a degree of optimism about the possibility of change.
- This model of intervention appeared to be less successful in work with families whose problems were both long-standing and severe.

Similarly, some North American studies have found that short-term, intensive preventive services are more successful where there are less difficult problems and where abuse and neglect are not chronic (Szykula and Fleischman, 1985; Nelson and others, 1988). In Britain, too, concerns have been expressed that, in work with teenagers, the emphasis on more immediate problems tends to neglect their more fundamental needs (DoH, 1996). With some families short-term interventions can bring, at most, only short-term solutions. Nevertheless, although many problems are not amenable to total resolution, single or successive short-term interventions may meet the needs of some young people and help their families through crises. In many cases, liaison with other agencies such as education and health will be needed to ensure that support to the family continues and, for some, follow-up support by social workers may also be necessary.

Some young people, however, are likely to need more than this if they are to remain at home and it is questionable whether short-term interventions by support teams alone can be of real benefit in these circumstances. Realistically, in some families, long-term underlying problems may be intractable, for example, where parents have serious mental health or substance abuse problems or children's behaviour problems are associated with long histories of neglect. In these circumstances, preventive work with young people may need to be sustained. Support team staff could have an important role as mentors to the young people, building up trust and respect over a longer period of time than is normally allotted for their work (DoH, 1996). However, support team staff are expected to build relationships and work effectively with young people along time-scales driven by agency needs to manage resources and contain costs, rather than by the young people's needs. Nevertheless, it is likely that longer-term support to young people from families with chronic and severe problems would, if successful, be less costly to social services than looking after them, although the cost spread across all the agencies involved in supporting such families may be quite high.

Direct work

Adolescent support teams serve an important function in offering direct work with young people and their parents. With social services provision often based on a quasi-market model, whereby the purchasing or commissioning of services is separated from service provision, greater specialisation has led to a fragmentation of the social work task (Freeman, 1999; Parton, 1997). As social workers find their role redefined as primarily one of case management, their work becomes increasingly focused on the management and coordination of resources and, as a result, they have fewer opportunities for direct work with young people. In contemporary children's services, this fragmentation of social work responsibilities may mean that much direct work with teenagers is hived off to specialist support teams. As we have seen, many of the young people and parents in this study valued highly the direct work undertaken with them. They felt that the team's negotiation and mediation skills helped them to resolve family problems, and the sense of being supported in dealing with their problems made some of them feel greater confidence in their capacity to address these problems. One of the benefits of specialisation was that the team had the opportunity to develop skills and experience in engaging young people and working with them in an informal, participative manner.

However, young people who came from families with severe and intractable problems were often more wary of engagement with professionals, but the time-scale on which the support team operated was too short to enable them to gain the young people's trust and build relationships with them. Also, some of these young people might have benefited from work that addressed their complex, underlying problems as well as the immediate problems that had precipitated referral to the team. However, not all the support team had the training or professional background to enable them to work in depth with young people, and many of the young people did not have allocated social workers who might potentially have done this work with them.

Assessment

The information gathered in assessments was often limited, particularly if they were undertaken by duty social workers. The assessments underpinning referrals to the team were often narrow in focus and did not include attention to young people's longer-term histories or needs. A balance needs to be struck between gathering information rapidly in order to meet young people's immediate needs and giving fuller consideration to the assessment of those young people with more complex needs (Sinclair and others, 1995). It is to be hoped that the new Department of Health consultation draft, *Framework for the Assessment of Children in Need and their Families* might lead to more comprehensive assessments and greater emphasis on planning a coordinated service (DoH, 1999b).

Assessments carried out solely by social workers were not always grounded in a sufficient appreciation of the potential role of other staff. The findings of this study suggest that joint assessment might be beneficial, involving both social workers and support team staff. Young people who might benefit from short-term direct work by the support team could be referred rapidly and, since assessment and intervention often overlap in work with young people in crisis, this work could begin at once. Also, since school problems were evident in nearly three-quarters of all preventive referrals, the secondment of an education social worker to adolescent support teams could help to ensure a coordinated approach to addressing problems both at home and at school. Similarly, the involvement of a housing support worker in joint assessment of the young homeless might ensure a better coordinated service. The housing support worker could then undertake the time-consuming work involved in finding accommodation, thus freeing the team to make better use of their social work skills in supporting homeless young people.

Coordination of services

As we have stressed, a coordinated approach to family support is vital, particularly where young people and families have chronic problems and multiple needs. Partnership with other professionals is one of the key principles underpinning the Children Act 1989, yet too often we found that different services made separate interventions with little joint planning. Within a framework of well-coordinated services, an adolescent support team might do focused work addressing problems of behaviour, parenting and family interaction, as part of a broader inter-agency plan for family support. For example, most of the young people referred for preventive work displayed disruptive behaviour at school or were non-attenders, which increased family stress. Coordination with professionals in the education service might have helped to reinforce and prolong any positive effects of intervention but, in practice, this rarely happened. In particular, where family problems were perceived as being less severe, there were no allocated social workers to undertake this liaison task and, as the support team were not the caseholders, they were not responsible for liaison either. In the two cases where regular inter-agency planning and review did take place, there was a greater coherence in the family support offered and the specific role of the support team within this was clear.

Avoiding accommodation in public care

In the context of local changes in policy and resources, which were informed both by professional child care concerns and by considerations of cost, social workers appeared to be more concerned with avoiding the need for accommodation than with avoiding family breakdown. As we have seen, although only two of the young people referred for preventive work were accommodated in public care, family breakdown occurred in a quarter of all preventive referrals during the year. Most of these young people moved out to stay with friends or relatives.

Social workers and support team staff were rightly concerned to avoid the unnecessary separation of young people from their families, and hoped that the provision of an alternative community-based service by the support team might resolve problems. However, there will always be circumstances in which the provision of accommodation, as part of a broader plan for family support, is the most appropriate option. A reluctance to provide this service may perhaps lead young people to make unplanned moves to stay with friends or relatives. For some, a stay with close relatives or family friends may be preferable to accommodation by the local authority, but a number of the young people who left home in this way in our study were living with a variety of friends in uncertain circumstances and one eventually became homeless.

In most cases, these moves to friends or relatives were not planned and, worryingly, once the young people had left home, there were delays in providing follow-up support, or no support was provided at all. These ad hoc arrangements were simply accepted, pending an assessment to approve them as private fostering arrangements. In some cases, there appeared to be an implicit assumption that the problem for social services was now resolved, whereas the young people might well have benefited from intervention to help them either to work towards returning home or to plan for a longer-term alternative.

The cost of preventive work with young people

The cost analysis presented in this study provides valuable budgetary information for service providers and highlights significant distinctions in the patterns of care received by young people at risk of entry into local authority care or accommodation and those who are homeless. Although the two groups of young people were found to incur similar costs over the study period – £123 versus £129 per week respectively – the input of each service-providing sector differed greatly. In respect of the prevention group, the total costs were borne almost entirely by social services, through the input of the support team and the education sector. In contrast, the total costs of services to the homeless group were shared more equally between the support team, other social services (particularly accommodation costs), youth custody and the NHS, with relatively little input from the education sector.

A full economic evaluation, involving the comparison of two or more alternatives in terms of both costs and benefits, was beyond the scope of this study. Thus, the relative effectiveness and cost effectiveness of the support team cannot be determined. To guide the inevitable choices between alternative services, future research should be encouraged to incorporate full comparative economic evaluations, for which the costing methodology described in this study provides a useful framework (see Appendix 1). Only in this way will it be possible to maximise the benefit young people gain from the resources available to social services departments.

12 Conclusion

Young people in different circumstances clearly have different support needs, yet decisions about the service stream they are allocated to may depend more on their age and the nature of the presenting problems at referral than on their needs. Once allocated to an adolescent support team, they are likely to receive a short-term, task-centred service. In the authority studied, this service appeared to be more successful with young people with less entrenched family problems and correspondingly less successful with those from families with chronic and severe problems. While direct work by the team was much appreciated and appeared to benefit some young people and parents, the immediate problems of the young people were more likely to receive attention than any more complex needs that they might have had. The team sometimes worked in isolation from other services and coordination with the work of other professionals was less likely to take place if there was no social worker allocated to the young person.

Socio-ecological perspectives on working with children with behaviour problems argue that young people's problems should be understood in terms of the key social contexts for adolescents: the family; the school; the peer group; and the neighbourhood. These theories suggest that not only parenting behaviour, but also the neighbourhood environment and the peer group all interact with child characteristics and have an effect on child behaviour. When families are under stress, changing characteristics of the child, for example during adolescence, may place them under additional strain (Borduin, 1994; Buysse, 1997; Cox, 1997).

Socio-ecological theories highlight the importance of an integrated approach, which addresses risk factors in different areas of a child's social networks. The implication of this model is that interventions should coordinate work in different areas of the young person's life – principally at home and at school – and reduce stresses for the parent so they can reinforce more direct preventive efforts. This may also involve linking families to informal support networks within communities, including community-based neighbourhood groups. For young people with severe problems, coordinated family support – involving support teams, social workers, education and health professionals, and the voluntary sector – may be needed to enhance any protective factors in their home, school and wider environment.

A more coherent inter-disciplinary approach is needed, particularly in work with young people from families where problems are chronic and severe. For many young people coming to the attention of social services, interventions may need to address problems in more than one context, so it is vital that interventions by different professionals are coordinated. The implication of this is that more attention should be given to initial assessment, and this should involve staff from other agencies where appropriate. Yet individual agencies may be reluctant to target resources on preventive services since, as the Social Exclusion Unit has argued, the rewards of effective prevention do not always fall on the organisation that was responsible for producing it. The Unit recommends a new ring-fenced preventive budget to improve support to families and promote effective cross-cutting interventions for young people (Social Exclusion Unit, 1999). Preventive services for teenagers should be part of a continuum of inter-agency family support services, which could identify the causes of early behavioural problems and respond to these as they emerge. For some young people, at least, this may prevent the development of acute problems in early adolescence which may result in their entry into public care.

Within this framework, inter-agency youth teams could be developed to work within and across agencies. Multi-disciplinary teams could operate from a central site and carry out assessments on young people who are deemed to be 'children in need'. Social services, housing and education could all second staff to the team, which would be managed by a multi-agency management board. Existing adolescent support team staff would have a central role in such teams, but they would be able to work in a more integrated way with colleagues from education and housing, as well as social workers seconded to the team. Decisions about who should be involved in responding to young people's needs, how their work should be coordinated and the proposed duration of the intervention could then follow from the assessment of a young person's needs rather than the point of entry to the service.

During this assessment, staff from existing adolescent support teams would have an important role to play in providing an immediate response to the crises which often precipitate referral. With their specialist skills and experience in working with adolescents, they would also contribute to the joint assessment and to further work, in some instances, taking the sole or principal role in the intervention and, in others, working alongside other professionals who might take on the key support role. For some young people, their problem-focused, action-oriented interventions may be sufficient to bring about shifts in young people's behaviour and family functioning, in the short term at least. With other young people, this approach may form one element of a coordinated inter-disciplinary service, which also provides follow-up support to those who need it. A similar model – a multi-skill support service – has been proposed by the Social Exclusion Unit to end institutional fragmentation in education and training support to 16- to 18-year-olds (Social Exclusion Unit, 1999). Multidisciplinary youth teams would offer joined-up services for adolescents in different circumstances and with different needs, developing a continuum of services for young people.

Appendix I Methodology

Monitoring

The work of the support team was monitored by means of analysis of their case files during the year 1 April 1998 to 31 March 1999, covering a total of 56 cases. All referrals for preventive work (37) or homelessness (19) were included, but not those for aftercare work. Data was extracted from the initial referral forms sent to the team by social workers, the agreement forms completed by support workers and young people, the running record and the team's progress reports and closure reports. Data was entered on a database and a thematic analysis was carried out.

Focus groups and key informant interviews

Focus groups were held in the early stages of the study with the support team and with both social work teams dealing with young people aged 11 and over. Key informant interviews were also undertaken with the senior children's services manager responsible for the team and with the two social work team managers.

Qualitative study

Twenty young people were interviewed, together with their support team worker, field social worker (if any) and one or both parents, if the young person was in contact with them and agreed to this. In total, twenty young people and support team staff were interviewed. In eleven cases, parents were interviewed and, in five cases, field social workers were also interviewed. The interviews were tape-recorded and transcribed.

The first round of interviews was carried out shortly after the support team's first contact with the young person, while the second stage interviews took place one month after case closure. The time between the first and follow-up interviews ranged from ten to 41 weeks and the average time that elapsed was 20 weeks. Four of the young people could not be traced at the second stage, although interviews were still carried out with their support workers at this point. All of these were homeless young people whose transient lifestyles meant that it was difficult for social services staff to maintain contact with them, unless they themselves chose to get in touch.

The qualitative sample was broadly stratified into two-thirds preventive cases and one-third homeless cases, in order to reflect the work of the team. Within this stratification, there were no selection criteria and those interviewed were the first twenty young people who agreed to take part in the study. A further nine refused to take part, whose mean age was just over a year younger than the mean for the monitoring sample.

Following an initial content analysis of the transcribed interviews, thematic indexing categories were devised to allow a cross-sectional analysis of cases. These included both descriptive and conceptual categories. In order to ensure that the complexity inherent in each individual account was not lost during the cross-sectional analysis of themes, 'slices' of text coded under thematic categories were accompanied by notes giving relevant contextual information about the particular circumstances of each young person. This strategy aimed to ensure that the cross-sectional thematic interpretation of the entire data set was informed by an holistic appreciation of the context and circumstances of each individual.

Evaluating outcomes

Data on outcomes of work with the monitoring sample was collected from case records at case closure. Information on outcomes for the interview sample was gathered at the follow-up interview one month after case closure. The choice of any follow-up period for assessing outcomes is problematic. In this instance, it was partly dictated by the time-scale of the study and partly by the fact that the support team was offering short-term, focused interventions whose effects could be expected to be measurable in the short-term. As the team was only in an early stage of its development when the evaluation was conducted, the discussion of outcomes may give some indication of the kinds of outcomes adolescent support teams might achieve but this should not be regarded as definitive.

The monitoring data is based solely on the views of support team staff, since it was drawn from the team's case records, so this is used only to assess young people's material circumstances at follow-up. In contrast, the qualitative data is based on the views of young people, parents, social workers and support team staff expressed in in-depth interviews. Since this data reflects the perspectives of all key players involved, it is used to assess the quality of life as well as the material circumstances of the young people after case closure.

The outcome dimensions measured were derived from the formal aims of the team and the goals of the work in individual cases: preventing accommodation; preventing family or placement breakdown; reducing conflict between young people and their parents or carers; and improving young people's behaviour, family relationships and communication. Outcomes for young people were compared to a baseline represented by their circumstances at the point of referral.

Costing methodology

Unit costs

The unit costs of services used were for the financial year 1998/99 and were derived from a number of different sources, including service providers, calculation from relevant salary scales and national publications (Chartered Institute of Public Finance and Accountancy, 1998; HM Prison Service, 1999; Netten and others, 1998). Published unit costs were inflated to 1998/99 prices where necessary using the Retail Price Index (Office for National Statistics, 1999). All unit costs (or ranges of costs) and the sources of these unit costs are detailed in Table 5 on p. 98.

Costing the support team

Two methods of calculating the input of the support team were employed:

I. Top-down (or average) estimation

The average cost per young person is calculated by dividing the total annual budget for the support team by the total number of allocated referrals during a one-year period. Information was available on the number of allocated referrals in each referral category (prevention, homelessness and leaving care) and the percentage of time the team spent on each category over the one-year period, thus it was possible to calculate an average cost per prevention case and per homelessness case.

2. Bottom-up (or micro-costing) estimation

The time team workers spent on each individual case was calculated, with non-case-specific work being allocated equally across all referrals. An hourly cost per worker was calculated on the basis of 1998/99 budgetary information and multiplied by the total number of hours allocated to each case, to provide a total cost per case.

Bottom-up estimations are generally considered to be more appropriate than top-down approaches as they take into consideration the fact that individuals use variable amounts of a service, rather than providing a fixed average cost per young person irrespective of the quantity of service received (Drummond and others, 1997). Bottom-up estimations, however, rely on the collection of accurate data on both case-specific and non-case-specific work and are therefore subject to the problems of data availability and data errors. As a check on accuracy, both methods were employed.

Table 6 on p. 99 details the total mean cost and cost per week of the support team per young person. On average, the top-down and bottom-up approaches differed little, strengthening the confidence we can have in the accuracy of the bottom-up cost estimations. Since bottom-up estimations more accurately reflect the true cost of a service for each individual, the analyses contained in the chapter on cost analysis (Chapter 10) refer only to the bottom-up estimation.

Substitute services

All young people expect to receive a certain number of services, such as a basic level of education. It was assumed in this study that these services are equal for all young people and thus only the cost of services considered to be additional to this basic minimum were included in the analysis. In some situations, however, services are in fact substitutes for this basic level of care, rather than additional to, and an adjustment to the cost of these services becomes necessary. For example, young people who have been excluded from school and attend a pupil support unit full time incur the additional cost of the pupil support unit, but also save the cost of mainstream school attendance. In such circumstances, the cost of an mainstream school place should be subtracted from the cost of the pupil support unit, to adjust for the fact that the young person is receiving a substitute service, rather than an additional service.

In this study, no such adjustments were made due to a lack of information on the nature of pupil support unit attendance. Two of the four young people who attended the unit were part-time students for whom the unit is likely to be additional to mainstream school attendance, and therefore no adjustment was necessary. The remaining two attended the pupil support unit five days a week during the period of the study, but no information was available to ascertain whether this attendance was temporary and thus whether a school place was being held open for them elsewhere. Adjustment was felt premature in the circumstances, but future evaluations should be aware of the distinction between additional and substitute services and make adjustments to costs where necessary.

Social security benefits

From the societal point of view, social security benefits (or transfer payments) are neither a cost nor a gain, but a transfer of money from one sector in society to another that does not involve any consumption of resources (Drummond and others, 1997). As the preferred viewpoint of the economist is societal, it is common for such benefits to be excluded from economic analyses. When the selected viewpoint is narrower, however, researchers may prefer to include such benefits in order to determine, for example, the total cost to the statutory sectors alone.

Although transfer payments were not included in this analysis, it is likely that some of the homeless young people were receiving housing benefits, for example, thus the costs to the statutory sectors alone would be higher than those reported here. However, from the societal point of view, the total costs reported would not differ. It is thus important for the perspective of an economic evaluation to be clearly identified in any future evaluation and the inclusion of social security benefits to be viewed with some caution.

Appendix 2 Tables

Table 1: Mean use of services by all young people during contact with support team

Service	All young people (n=16)	
	mean	range
Support team:		
Support team worker hours	31.4	9–63
Other social services:		
Social work contacts	2.3	0–17
Supported accommodation days	12.3	0–75
Foster care days	0.0	n/a
Residential care days	0.0	n/a
Education services:		
Education social worker contacts	7.0	0–80
Educational psychologist contacts	1.8	0–19
Classroom support days	7.7	0–60
Pupil support centre days	14.4	0–96
Training schemes/college-based services	2.4	0–32
NHS services:		
GP contacts	0.8	0–5
Practice nurse contacts	0.8	0–5
Inpatient days	0.4	0–4
Outpatient attendances	0.1	0–2
A&E attendances	0.4	0–2
Physiotherapist contacts	0.3	0–4
School doctor contacts	0.1	0–1
School nurse contacts	0.8	0–12
Voluntary services:		
Advice/counselling contacts	0.2	0–2
Youth custody:		
Youth custody days	1.9	0–31
Youth custody social work contacts	1.5	0–24

Table 2: Mean use of services during contact with support team by status

Service	Prevention (n=12)		Homeless (n=4)	
	mean	range	mean	range
Support team:				
Support team worker hours	33.3	21–57	25.8	9–63
Other social services:				
Social work contacts	2.7	0–17	1.0	0–4
Supported accommodation days	0.0	n/a	49.3	0–75
Foster care days	0.0	n/a	0.0	n/a
Residential care days	0.0	n/a	0.0	n/a
Education services:				
Education social worker contacts	9.3	0–80	0.3	0–1
Educational psychologist contacts	2.3	0–19	0.0	n/a
Classroom support days	10.3	0–60	0.0	n/a
Special needs unit days	19.3	0–96	0.0	n/a
Training schemes/college-based services	0.2	0–2	9.3	0–32
NHS services:				
GP contacts	0.7	0–4	1.3	0–5
Practice nurse contacts	0.1	0–1	2.8	0–5
Inpatient days	0.0	n/a	1.6	0–4
Outpatient attendances	0.0	n/a	0.5	0–2
A&E attendances	0.5	0–2	0.3	0–2
Physiotherapy contacts	0.0	n/a	1.0	0–4
School doctor contacts	0.1	0–1	0.0	n/a
School nurse contacts	1.1	0–12	0.0	n/a
Voluntary services:				
Advice/counselling contacts	0.3	0–2	0.0	n/a
Youth custody:				
Youth custody days	0.0	n/a	7.8	0–31
Youth custody social work contacts	0.0	n/a	6.0	0–24

Table 3: Mean cost of all services during contact with support team (£)

Service	All young people (n=16)		Prevention (n=12)		Homeless (n=4)	
	mean cost (SD)	% of total cost	mean cost (SD)	% of total cost	mean cost (SD)	% of total cost
Support team	1106 (317)	45	1166 (271)	50	926 (420)	32
Other social services	206 (374)	8	58 (111)	2	649 (551)	22
Total social services	1312 (295)	53	1224 (255)	52	1575 (268)	54
Education sector	858 (1249)	35	1078 (1380)	46	197 (197)	7
NHS	155 (392)	6	34 (35)	2	519 (728)	18
Voluntary sector	4 (12)	0	5 (14)	0	0 (0)	0
Youth custody	156 (601)	6	0 (0)	0	602 (1204)	21
Total	2485 (1572)	100	2341 (1439)	100	2893 (2114)	100

Table 4: Mean cost of all services per week (£)

Service	All young people (n=16)		Prevention (n=12)		Homeless (n=4)	
	mean cost per week (SD)	% of total cost	mean cost per week (SD)	% of total cost	mean cost per week (SD)	% of total cost
Support team	55.21 (21.45)	44	60.61 (22.06)	49	39.00 (19.62)	30
Other social services	10.89 (20.52)	9	3.11 (6.31)	3	34.23 (31.48)	27
Total social services	66.10 (23.70)	53	63.72 (22.46)	52	73.23 (29.48)	57
Education sector	44.61 (77.71)	36	57.16 (86.82)	46	6.97 (6.08)	5
NHS	7.44 (17.07)	6	1.85 (2.30)	2	24.19 (30.64)	19
Voluntary sector	0.12 (0.33)	0	0.16 (0.38)	0	0.00 (0.00)	0
Youth custody	6.43 (24.88)	5	0.00 (0.00)	0	24.92 (49.85)	19
Total	124.70 (89.07)	100	122.89 (93.03)	100	129.31 (88.88)	100

Table 5: 1998/99 unit costs

Service	Unit cost or range (£)	Unit	Source
Support team:			
Top-down	1131	per prevention case	Service provider
	809	per homeless case	Service provider
Bottom-up	640–1740	per child	Service provider
Other social services:			
Social work	22	per hour of client-related work	PSSRU
Supported accommodation	6–16	per day	Service provider
Education services:			
Education social worker	22	per hour	PSSRU
Educational psychologist	25	per hour	Salary scales
Classroom support	13	per hour	Salary scales
Pupil support centre	32	per day	Service provider
NHS services:			
GP	10	per surgery consultation	PSSRU
Practice nurse	7	per surgery consultation	PSSRU
Inpatient	193–318	per day	CIPFA
Outpatient	48	per attendance	CIPFA
A&E	37	per attendance	CIPFA
Physiotherapy	30	per hour of client contact	PSSRU
School doctor	26	per hour	Salary scales
School nurse	15	per hour	Salary scales
Voluntary services:			
Advice/counselling	22	per hour of client-related work	PSSRU
Youth custody:			
Youth custody	61	per day	HM Prison Service
Youth custody social work	22	per hour of client-related work	PSSRU

PSSRU – Personal Social Services Research Unit (Netten and others, 1998); CIPFA – Chartered Institute of Public Finance and Accountancy (CIPFA, 1998); HM Prison Service (HM Prison Service, 1999).

Table 6: Mean cost of the support team (£)

	Top-down estimation	Bottom-up estimation
All young people (n=16):		
Mean cost of support team	1051	1106
Range	809–1131	640–1740
Mean cost per week	55.5	55.2
Prevention (n=12):		
Mean cost of support team	1131	1166
Range	1131	914–1740
Mean cost per week	61.5	60.6
Homeless (n=4):		
Mean cost of support team	809	927
Range	809	640–1546
Mean cost per week	37.5	39.0

References

Aldgate, J and Tunstill, J (1995) *Making Sense of Section 17.* HMSO

Audit Commission (1994) *Seen but not Heard.* Audit Commission

Audit Commission (1996) *Misspent Youth ... Young People and Crime.* Audit Commission

Bebbington, A and Miles, J (1989) 'The background of children who enter local authority care', *British Journal of Social Work*, 19, 349–68

Besharov, D (1994) 'Looking beyond 30, 60 and 90 days', *Children and Youth Services Review*, 16, 445–51

Biehal, N and Wade, J (1999) '"I thought it would be easier": The early housing careers of young people leaving care', *in* Rugg, J *ed. Young People, Housing and Social Policy.* Routledge

Borduin, C (1994) 'Innovative models of treatment and service delivery in the juvenile justice system', *Journal of Clinical Child Psychology*, 23 (suppl), 19–25

Brown, J (1998) *Family and Adolescent Support Service*, Draft discussion paper. National Institute of Social Work

Buchanan, A and Ten Brinke, J (1998) 'Measuring outcomes for children: early parenting experiences, conflict, maladjustment and depression in adulthood', *Children and Youth Services Review*, 20, 3, 251–78

Buysse, W (1997) 'Behaviour problems and relationships with family and peers during adolescence', *Journal of Adolescence*, 20, 6, December 1997, 645–59

Chartered Institute of Public Finance and Accountancy (1998) *The Health Service Financial Database 1998.* Chartered Institute of Public Finance and Accountancy

Cleaver, H, Unell, I and Aldgate, J (1999) *Children's Needs: Parenting Capacity. The impact of parental mental illness, problem alcohol and drug use and domestic violence on children's development.* The Stationery Office

Cleaver, H and Freeman, P (1995) *Parental Perspectives in Cases of Suspected Child Abuse.* The Stationery Office

Colton, M, Drury, C, Williams, M (1995) *Children in Need: Family Support under the Children Act 1989*. Avebury

Cox, A (1997) 'Preventing child abuse: a review of community projects: intervening on processes and outcome of reviews', *Child Abuse Review*, 6, 243–56

Craig, T, Hodson, S, Woodward, S and Richardson, S (1996) *Off to a Bad Start*. Mental Health Foundation

Department of Health (1995) *Child Protection: Messages from Research*. HMSO

Department of Health (1996) *Focus on Teenagers*. HMSO

Department of Health (1998a) *Quality Protects: Framework for Action*, Department of Health

Department of Health (1998b) *Modernising Health and Social Services: National Priorities Guidance 1999/00–2000/02*. Department of Health

Department of Health (1999a) *Children Looked After by Local Authorities. Year Ending 31 March 1998*. Department of Health

Department of Health (1999b) *Framework for the Assessment of Children in Need and their Families (Consultation Draft)*. Department of Health

Drummond, M F, O'Brien, B, Stoddart, G L, Torrance, G W (1997) *Methods for the Economic Evaluation of Health Care Programmes*. Oxford Medical Publications

Evans, A (1996) *'We Don't Choose To Be Homeless.' Report of the National Enquiry into Preventing Youth Homelessness*. CHAR

Farmer, E and Parker, R (1991) *Trials and Tribulations*. The Stationery Office

Fisher, M, Marsh, P and Phillips, D (1986) *In and Out of Care*. Batsford/British Agencies for Adoption and Fostering

Fraser, M, Pecora, P and Haapala, D (1991) *Families in Crisis: The impact of intensive family preservation Services*. Aldine de Gruyter

Freeman, R (1999) 'Recursive politics: prevention, modernity and social systems.' *Children and Society*, 13, 232–41

Frost, N (1997) 'Delivering family support: issues and themes in service development' *in* Parton, N ed. *Child Protection and Family Support*. Routledge

Graham, J and Bowling, B (1995) *Young People and Crime: Research Study 145*. Home Office

HM Prison Service (1999) *Annual Report and Accounts April 1998 to March 1999*. The Stationery Office

Howe, D (1996) 'Surface and depth in social work practice' *in* Parton, N ed. (1996) *Social Theory, Social Change and Social Work*. Routledge

Jack, G and Jordan, B (1999) 'Social capital and child welfare', *Children and Society*, 13, 242–56

Jones, G (1995) *Leaving Home*. Open University Press

Kay, H (1994) *Conflicting Priorities*. CHAR/Institute of Housing

London Research Centre (1996) *Estimates of Young Single Homelessness – A Report to NCH Action for Children*. NCH Action For Children

McCluskey, J (1993) *Re-assessing Priorities. The Children Act 1989 – A new agenda for young homeless people?* CHAR

Nelson, K, Emlen, A, Landsman, M and Hutchinson, J (1988) *Family-Based Services: Factors contributing to success and failure in family-based welfare services*. University of Iowa

Netten, A, Dennett, J and Knight, J (1998) *Unit Costs of Health and Social Care*. PSSRU, University of Kent at Canterbury

Office for National Statistics (1999) *Consumer Trends: The first quarter 1999*. The Stationery Office

Packman, J, Randall, J and Jaques, N (1986) *Who Needs Care?* Blackwell

Packman, J and Hall, C (1998) *From Care to Accommodation*. The Stationery Office

Parton, N (1997) 'Child protection and family support: current debates and future prospects' *in* Parton, N ed. *Child Protection and Family Support*. Routledge

Pawson, R and Tilley, N (1994) 'What works in evaluation research?' *British Journal of Criminology*, 34, 3, 291–306

Pecora, P, Fraser, M, Nelson, J, McCroskey, J and Meezan, W (1995) *Evaluating Family-Based Services*. Aldine de Gruyter

Pleace, N and Quilgars, D (1999) 'Youth homelessness' *in* Rugg, J ed. *Young People, Housing and Social Policy*. Routledge

Rees, G and Stein, M (1997) 'Abuse of adolescents: implications of North American research for the UK', *Children and Society*, 11, 128–34

Reid, W and Epstein, (1972) *Task-Centred Casework*. New York: Columbia University Press

Rodgers, B and Pryor, J (1998) *Divorce and Separation: The outcomes for children*, Joseph Rowntree Foundation

Rowe, J, Hundleby, M and Garnett, L (1989) *Child Care Now*. Batsford/BAAF

Rutter, M and Smith, D (eds) (1995) *Psychosocial Disorders In Young People: Time Trends and their Causes*. Chichester: Wiley

Schuerman, J, Rzepnicki, T and Littell, J (1994) *Putting Families First: An experiment in family preservation*. Aldine de Gruyter

Scott, S (1998) 'Fortnightly review: aggressive behaviour in childhood', *British Medical Journal*, 316, 202–6

Sinclair, I and Gibbs, I (1998) *Children's Homes. A Study in Diversity*. Wiley

Sinclair, R, Garnet, L, Berridge, D (1995) *Social Work and Assessment with Adolescents*. National Children's Bureau

Sinclair, R, Hearn, B and Pugh, G (1997) *Preventive Work with Families: The role of mainstream services*. National Children's Bureau

Smith, J, Gilford, S and O'Sullivan, A (1998) *The Family Background of Young Homeless People*. Family Policy Studies Centre

Social Exclusion Unit (1999) *Bridging the Gap: New opportunities for 16- to 18-year-olds not in education, employment or training*. The Stationery Office

Social Exclusion Unit (2000): *Report of Policy Action Team 12: Young People*. The Stationery Office

Szykula, S and Fleischman, M (1985) 'Reducing out of home placements of abused children: two controlled field studies', *Child Abuse and Neglect*, 9, 277–83

Triseliotis, J, Borland, M, Hill, M and Lambert, L (1995) *Teenagers and the Social Work Services*. The Stationery Office

Wade, J and Biehal, N (1998) *Going Missing: Young people absent from care*. Wiley

Wells, K and Biegel, D (1991) *Family Preservation Services*. Sage

Index

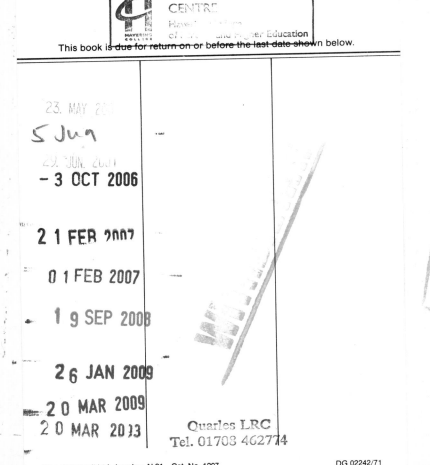